Ulysses S. Grant

Five-Star General and Eighteenth President

Ulysses S. Grant

PRIMOGENITOR OF AMERICAN CIVIL PROPRIETY

A RESOURCEFUL, VENTURESOME, CONSCIENTIOUS, EQUITABLE, GENEROUS, RESOLUTE, and GUTSY HERO

Thomas Edward Grant, PhD

ISBN: 1547024909
ISBN 13: 9781547024902
Library of Congress Control Number: 2017908628
CreateSpace Independent Publishing Platform
North Charleston, South Carolina

A Four-Hundredth-Year

American Family

Commemorative Erudition

Circa AD 1620 to AD 2020

My family is American, and has been for generations, in all its branches, direct and collateral.

—Personal Memoirs of Ulysses S. Grant

Contents

Preface

ULYSSES S. GRANT CONTINUES TO be the subject of American writers long after his life. Some have written that he was simple. Some have written that he was no match for Lee. Some have written that he was a butcher. Some have written that he was a poor judge of men. Some have written that he was a drunk. Some have even written that he was a "nobody from nowhere."

Grant continues to be the subject of so much interest and so many myths perhaps because the man was actually unusually complex rather than simple, a superior match for Lee, not a butcher, not a poor judge of men, and not of course, "Nobody from nowhere."

Many writers have ascribed pejorative traits to Ulysses S. Grant, but nobody to date has truly, or instinctively known the man. A real key to understanding Ulysses S. Grant, is in the context of the nature and nurture of a remarkable American family.

CHAPTER 1

Providence

American Brands, Plucky Leadership, and the Cam Stroke:
Canons of Order versus Certain Chaos

EMERGING FROM THE PEOPLE BORN, parented, and raised solely within the first generations of America came a reflective family philosopher in war and in peace, a vulnerable but plucky military and moral icon of the nineteenth century, and at the age of forty-six, the eighteenth president of the United States. This unassuming but perceptive and righteous person came from the bleeding edge and geographical center of his up-and-coming country with the right balance of moral sensitivity and firmness to become the aptly nicknamed U. S. Grant, the singular most trusted champion of the Republic, and a truly devoted husband and father of his time.

As I begin this closely held commemoration of general and president Ulysses S. Grant from a family perspective, it is now more fittingly discernible that the peculiar way events distinctly manifest throughout New England often trend from the nation's enlightened and energized heartland. No matter how extraordinary an event has been here, it has often been forcefully preceded by not-so-uncommon disturbances there. To the classic New Englander, this may not always have been apparent, but in retrospect and from a distance, one can now clearly see that the auspicious momentum of restless pioneers was steadfastly implanted into the wilds of the Western Reserve, causing the detection of many a fracas from that booming territory, ranging from the capricious changes of our already inconsistent weather to the dreadful Civil War and the genius of Grant.

Much has already been written acclaiming U. S. Grant's fame; his eminence in his own time as the first five-star general since George Washington, the "father of our country"; his popularity as "defender of the Union"; his implicit national service as the first US presidential protector in chief of America's most righteous values and dominant proprieties of life, and his status as the first potential three-term president as Americans consistently voted for identity and coherence in the form of Grant's personal integrity, stability, and propitious guarantee of the forcible maintenance of justice and peace. All this has been examined in many volumes, and many have helped and hindered over the years the consideration of what made a contemplative, outwardly serene, generous, often inconspicuous, visibly unpretentious, and tacitly poignant-appearing spirit so personally recognized, trusted, and empowered by the American people.

Abraham Lincoln said he believed that Grant had strong "pertinacity." The Civil War president defined this tacit characteristic as the ability to imagine the whole picture and to artfully determine what needed to be done to make it so. Lincoln saw Grant to be a fighter and wanted all his Union generals to take the fight to the Confederacy like Grant. "Honest Abe" is credited for having seriously considered an executive order to find out what whiskey and cigars Grant liked and to give those to all his generals. Instead, he chose to put Ulysses S. Grant in command.

Even Ulysses was mindful of the mounting mystery pertaining to recognition of his leadership, and he pointed to his invariable commitment to family—particularly his unremitting courtship of and fidelity to Julia, a delightful Southern girl who was the love of his life—and a keen implanted personal and professional devotion as the inclination for plainly "doing what you have to do."

Clearly Grant was alert to the conflict between north and south and was armed with certain rejoinders he thought to be persuasive and compelling in support for avoiding outright war between states. But once war was declared, Grant mustered, taught, and disciplined his own midwestern company of infantry volunteers for the impending fight even before he had been told to do so. He assumed command, trained his company, and then received recognition from the Ohio governor. He mulishly stuck to his own natural and provincial artistry, a brand of introspective but genial leadership.

Studying the fluky fate of any rapid rise to surefire renown is engaging, enlightening, and even numinous, no less so because our down-to-earth subject was a first-class family man. Julia and Ulysses carried out years of correspondence when he was involved with the war in Mexico, and she joined him at field headquarters during the Civil War when he allowed it. She supported him in all he was doing as her "knight." Likewise, he kept his family as close as possible as long as they could be securely out of harm's way.

What Ulysses's temperament and behavior were like is the least difficult aspect of his particular destiny to explain rationally. The difficulty he (and I, too) would have attempting to describe the inexplicable peculiarities that can shape a life, making it seem so set apart or supernaturally intended. For example, how does one explain all the instances in which that the bullets of enemies always physically missed their corporeal target, or the fact that one's own physical and spiritual propriety aroused a quirkily beguiling and disarming effect in potential mortal adversaries?

On November 24, 2016, one of our four grandsons was aiming and effortlessly launching a garden stake at overripe pumpkins, as any boy will do. Those pumpkins had enjoyed many better days, and a mildly threatening-looking, moderate-sized jack-o-lantern left over from Halloween became a primary focus of the fun. His parents and I were casually celebrating the favorite holiday and observing him closely. Some of the throws made by this precocious seven-year-old hit their target, and several completely missed, but we all cheered words of encouragement as the results would appropriately allow. Cameron hit the nasty-looking pumpkin firmly and squarely, and all his onlookers cheered this result. He pulled out the stake, leaving a small square hole in the center no bigger than the stake itself, or no more than a half-inch square. The boy was admired for striking this target so well, and, emboldened, he immediately threw the projectile once again. This time the cam stroke incredibly entered the exact same hole as squarely as did the first. Surprised, I excitedly cheered, "A bull's-eye!" Gathering self-control, I asked more seriously, "What do you think the chances are of striking the same small hole twice in exactly the same way?" Answering my own question, I affirmed, "That wouldn't *ever* happen!"

This led to my reflecting seriously that perhaps it was so with the subject of this book, Ulysses S. Grant. He was brave and consistent and accustomed to demonstrating first-rate aims and pertinent performance; he exalted straightforward humility, honesty, and facility, like those of a child prodigy, and he readily hit a "bull's-eye," at least in the imagination of the people, more often than not. He steadily exhibited an almost supernatural countenance, which added to his startling successes.

A strong sense of preeminence, incomparability, ascendancy, or right of destiny are remembered as a most firm and patent personal drive for living a quality life, or at least for perpetual testing of boundaries, examining and working around obstructions, and developing inherent hypotheses about personal providence. These qualities helped ignite early passion for a durable personal philosophy, one acquired by reflection on family trust, before I had learned too many unnecessary mundane, inconsistent, or unhappy minutiae that could have significantly hindered my impressionable imagination from engaging in the sensible pursuit of identifying meaningful aims and methods.

CHAPTER 2

The Great River

Origins of Connecticut, Prehistoric Cultural
Foundations, and the New World Stage and Vetting

FOR THE PAST FOUR OR five years, we have conscientiously worked the family garden (on a public plot measuring 432 square feet) within the town of Farmington's river plain, which was, geologically speaking, an ancient lake bottom until only several thousand years ago. The good soil found here is the product of recycled life. The people here, where we live now, simply call this the Farmington Meadows, or sometimes, insipidly, the "Farmington Flats."

The rich soil, a product of eons of living things, is certainly nothing to be passive and indifferent about. This is why I now bring it to your attention. The nutrient-rich land is perfect for repeated gardening, year after year; it allows for appropriate crop rotation, and any vegetable is normally capable of growing well here and probably has done so for the original inhabitants over hundreds if not several thousands of years. Fertile river plateaus are one certainly remarkable commonality both the Farmington River and the Great River share in common—these plateaus are almost literally as old as the hills, and they were certainly present when the first planters came here from Europe in 1633.

The Great River is, of course, the Connecticut River. Into it flow many significant smaller rivulets, like the Farmington, all along its entire length from Maine through New Hampshire, Vermont, Massachusetts, and Connecticut. For many centuries before this great river completely developed to its present form, native people inhabited the forested hills surrounding a large natural inland lake that supported an extensive intercultural trading terrain. As the body of water eventually forced its way through natural obstructions that were under extraordinary physical pressures, the several watercourses became fully separate and distinct features of the geography, and former islands and lower areas became successive connected plateaus of farmland.

Connecticut River, South Windsor, Feb. 2017

At the town of Deep River, Connecticut, for example, the exceptional river depth that colonists discovered was formed from the powerful activity of a prehistoric waterfall that gradually eroded a preexisting natural earthen dam. About thirty miles north, the great lake incrementally drained to the sea and fully articulated the ensuing riverbanks of the Connecticut and Farmington from one another.

Earlier human inhabitants of this greater lake region fished, hunted, farmed, and traded all along the wide and lengthy lake and riverbanks as the water imperceptibly receded over time to its present borders. These original people established their cultures and left behind impressive stone tools, artifacts, and works of art on the successive plateaus along the waterways over centuries as the great lake and its tributaries shrank silently but continuously on and on.

Leaving behind their objet d'art as many as fifteen thousand years ago, native peoples set out in dugout wooden canoes and traded from village to village across the Eastern Seaboard and inland to the heartland a thousand miles from the Atlantic. The first immigrants could put a vessel in the Great River and steer effortlessly southward with the river flow all the way from what we now call Maine through New England to Connecticut and to the Atlantic Ocean.

Transportation, industry, and travel throughout the vast prehistoric inland lake region were developed along the common pathways formed by an abundant diversity of animals and native humans—by all life forms that could have found the region home over the past 130 centuries. Perhaps five hundred generations of predecessors have inhabited this farmable region, if you consider that each compatible couple has raised a new family here every twenty-five years or so.

Weeds also grow exceptionally well, of course, here on the flats of the river plateau. They are ubiquitous. I mention this because even in the best circumstances, and despite the perfect intentions and plans, there is always something to test one's devotion, management ability, and endurance. A new gardener needs to try several strategies to eliminate the ubiquitous weeds—they appear to grow even more hardily than the finest plants. So I prefer planting fourteen to eighteen inches apart, not the customary twelve, and will run a small cultivator around the plants to destroy competing weeds at least two times during the summer growing season here from the end of April to late September.

To convince you it's worth the effort, I can tell you that we have successfully grown many delicious edible plants and herbs, including basil, lettuce, kale, heirloom tomatoes, broccoli, and varieties of peppers, squash, eggplant, and Butter and Sugar corn. Given favorable conditions, this small garden will produce enough food for a couple to consume awesome vegetables all summer and provide a satisfactory surplus to freeze and keep for the winter months.

In the middle and late sixteenth century, even before the English planters sought this region for their farms, explorers by land and sea inadvertently introduced horrible diseases to the originally healthy and strong indigenous people and culture of America. Diseases that arrived to this continent for the first time, were as lethal as the deadly plague, and swept through the Native Americans. This certainly happened a few years ahead of the first immigrant settlers and planters, and it was a primary reason the newcomers found an implausibly munificent abundance of freshly cleared land ready for their planting, and usually no one existing in sight with any considerable claim to it.

Second, altering alliances and numerous conflicts between the indigenous tribes continued to make peace and cooperation among the indigenous people a rare proceeding. In desperation, some River Indians looked to the English and an apparently fine foreign system of laws to settle serious disputes between intertribal factions in a fair and equitable way and forestall the continued customary retaliation. The colonial courts often failed to provide satisfactory results and were even carelessly indifferent to enforcement of law among the Indians. Colonial judges often ruled that the Indians settle their own differences and limited the extremes of violence and retribution only in locales controlled exclusively by the colonies.

The intolerable social disorder, along with the native people's lack of immunity from disease, triggered the obstinate, ironic, and satirical notion of cultural and religious invincibility among the ethnocentric immigrants. It seemed to the newcomers that all good things came from a feared god and that they alone were being favored as an elite to inherit this new, pure, still powerfully unspoiled land. Compatible religious devotion helped them to expediently reason that they had been led to a destiny for the purpose of taking possession, improving life on earth among men and nature, and living righteously by a new covenant with God in this "New England."

It is at the end of the Farmington River Valley, at the junction of the Farmington and the Great River, that the English from Dorchester first discovered a deforested, fertile, and virtually unclaimed land, plentiful much more than enough for their new settlement.

Mathew Grant, one such venturesome and pious Englishman, was the first to professionally survey the land to provide a two-acre parcel for each family willing and able to relocate from the original Dorchester settlement in Massachusetts Bay. This happened in 1633 and 1634, only three years after Grant and family made the daring voyage from Plymouth, England.

For just about any distinguished service to the colonies, large tracts of land were eventually granted to adventuresome men or simply taken through customary squatters' rights. Mathew surveyed and provided legitimate parcels of land on both sides of the Great River for farming and grazing livestock; the distribution of these parcels represented the orderly planning of Windsor, the first English settlement in Connecticut.

His development of "Windsor Farmes" on the Great River's east side, at East Windsor Hill, extended from the third and highest river plateau, descending a mile or two along wide natural river grassland that provided open space for grazing and farming near the edge of the river.

Enterprising people stimulated the development of an era of essential industry, labor, and commerce in the Connecticut River Valley that was unique, foreign, and typically almost incomprehensible to the Indians and their local cultural norms. As new land was developed for titled homesteads and farming communities were constituted, many occupations and careers blossomed into prosperous livelihoods for the new colonial Americans.

CHAPTER 3

Natural Synchronicity

Soldiers and Indians, Understanding with Empathy,
The Lost Art of Play, and Peaceful Witness

THE WEATHER AT THE BEGINNING of spring, specifically on April 30 in Connecticut, has typically been dry and around seventy-two degrees during the day, with nighttime rain that helps rejuvenate every thing living true to its quintessence. The agreeableness of cool dry omnipotent morning air inspires a renewed devotion and a feeling of comfort in those who have spent a good portion of their lives in the great outdoors and are filled with joy by natural discovery. I never sincerely appreciated the less engaged or less venturesome days. If I couldn't be outside, reasonably involved, and independently masterful, achieving this state was a glory of competence that I dreamed about regularly. In a classroom at school, for example, I remember listening to teachers with an oppositional or defiant sensibility, at best halfheartedly, amiably unaware and uninterested until the start of the fifth grade. But outside, I was a born observer and learned about everything organically, as life came along and things just happened. Processing everything with reflection came naturally, as does a pleasant surprise because of the awesome diversity and successful purpose of everything. If it was possible to walk or run into nature, I wanted to go see and be a part of it all without limits or sophistry.

There were no other kids on Forbes Street, East Hartford, Connecticut, where we lived years ago, so I played at imaginary adventures about cowboys and Indians, all alone until school age. I found it enjoyable to role-play by alternating between the Indian, the cowboy, and the horse. My only responsibility that I can recall was to be home by chow-time. I listened to my mother and took what she said very seriously. She would be very upset if I couldn't determine the time of day by looking at the position of the sun in the sky. And since the sun was always directly overhead at noon and at the same place at four o'clock every evening, I learned quickly to be home before I was called late for a meal. There was no good excuse for not being on time for the joy of eating. No kidding—those were the harmonious good old days as long as I was mentally and physically in sync with explicit and meaningful house rules.

Outside, each breath promised the reward of an ultimately benign, forgiving and sublime universe that worked peacefully in remarkable contrast, its formative diversity a treasure in its awesome and unbelievable abundance. I could spend more than one lifetime learning little-known facts and still find only unfathomable mysteries to excite reasoning and imagination. But there was always some consequential punishment with no actual damnation when behaving out of synch with propriety, or what I called at that time, "laws of nature." Outside discovery was always engaging, physically and mentally, and learning was certainly pleasant, too. I strongly perceived that there was a good reason for everything. It was my work, or at this age my active play, to always understand as much as possible of what I discovered including how everything ultimately resolved in harmony. It was also my responsibility to appreciate this honestly and amply.

This process of outside discovery has always favored the philosopher in me. I imagine the process as an inherent kind of learning, an education of its own. If we go back in history we observe that our ancestors had no other type of learning to know about this world. Only four hundred years ago, not many people could, or would, even read the Bible. Perhaps if we never had active play in childhood for exploration and discovery to identify the true principles of life, or what is consistent with the fundamental laws of nature, we would never have developed conventions like books or the social inventions of faith, religion, or education.

I made peculiar and straightforward assessment of many personal observations. Perception was often reality to me, at least in play. As a child I almost always thought, for example, that April 30th was ordinarily an unusually beautiful day. If there was ever just one day to be outside and positively focused on the spontaneous impressions about past and the future, for me it's truly always been this supernaturally wonderful day. This April 30th, my 66th birthday, has been particularly gracious and pleasant because I began to write this much-imagined, extraordinarily motivated, and at the very least self-entertaining commentary about the surprising samples of significant life that I've cherished, from the median moments of the twentieth century to the first quarter of the twenty-first century. As you will see soon enough, I will be seventy-one years of age when this book meets its publisher.

Ulysses Grant was born in April also. This no doubt explains a part of the personal affinity or unexpected serious metaphysical quirk I've experienced regarding him. He could well have understood also the same sense of existential spiritual rapture I always easily sensed and appreciated in late April. I wish that he had lived in my neighborhood and that we had grown to be friends as early as possible. What fun we could have had playing soldiers and Indians in sync with a rewarding magical world that the coordinated imaginations of two soldiers, or small boys, would have made together.

He lived in the nineteenth century, of course, but meaningful parallels in life that can be drawn from stories about him, and about other members of the family, either alike or unlike, are always attention grabbing and stirring to an alert imagination. It is enjoyable to compare time-enhanced innovations and features of lifestyles that are constantly becoming more meaningful, or fading, and then perhaps becoming more relevant again in not so many years. Individuals are fundamentally very much alike from one generation to another or even one continent to another. It seems that's the way it has been always, but it is hardly ever seen as such. Even the greatest celebrities and famous people are little different really. In the long run, even the most mundane and most important aspects of living organisms are in all ways related by diversity and synchronicity in opportunity and time.

In my study at home, I have established a library of books, found over the course of a little more than five decades to date at secondhand and contemporary bookstores, on the subjects of kindred discussed here. I have read all of them with intense interest at least once, and some two or more times for reasons to numerous to recall.

My interest in finding information on Ulysses S. Grant and other ancestors began at ten years of age and has continued to now because of a peculiar faculty and associated phenomena that actually demonstrated to me the breathtaking presence of previous centuries, particularly through reading of characters that were comfortable to relate to—Paul Revere, for example, and his brave spirit during Revolutionary War days.

Since beginning this new compilation of wonderful fiction and nonfiction reading material, I have come to believe that my chief advantage now as the author, if I can truthfully claim any, is having lived continuously in the place of my family's naturally obscured colonial origins, a place now replete with many almost completely hidden secrets about the fully forgotten originals of each generation. Each awesome and (I sometimes suspect) even perhaps divinely implanted hint is miraculously given up to a surprise awareness like that of a hidden message, or like some strange communication with a character who really only wants to be better known and finally, at last, a bit better understood, and rightfully appreciated.

Of course, I have considered that such incidents could very simply have developed as a coherent interpretation of independent and negligible coincidences and factual matter, with consequential links to understanding something great, or greater in perspective than my own mere separate, normal, and inconsequential identity. Normally I reasoned that I was being led somewhere important by most sensible hints, or telltale signs, of years of real life gone away. I have also always had a healthy amount of doubt about whatever I discovered, but then again, does not original research often rest on the preliminary premonition, or the strong gutsy hunch? So I may have been "called" to do this, but now it's the persistent distillation, or reduction to the simplest of alternatives, that in reality always carries the most weight.

The remnants of a small, close-knit, faithful, and economically vulnerable frontier family certainly witnessed the arrival of Hiram Ulysses Grant, his name at birth, 192 years after the family's first arrival in America in 1630. Ulysses Grant was presented to this world on April 27, 1822, on the gradual rise to a high point at the river plateau named Point Pleasant, Ohio. His first home was a one-room cabin made of timber from the many trees cleared there on site. These were some of the largest trees of an aboriginal forest that had matured on the highland near the great Ohio River.

After the passing of only 124 years and three days, I was also born and delivered in much the same manner, though this more recent event actually took place in a big eleven-story steel, cement, brick, and glass "skyscraper" called Hartford Hospital. This hospital was less than a mile from the great Connecticut River here. A bright new brownstone memorial archway honoring the heroic Ulysses S. Grant and his grand Union army had also been built here and had been dedicated with an elaborate orchestrated celebration only a few months earlier. This monument was an easy stroll less than a mile north on grounds near the Connecticut State capitol building. Several more miles north of the memorial, the contemporary suburban community of Windsor was an apt lifelong buttress on the subject of the brave and adventuresome past of the Grant forbearers and the founders of Connecticut Colony in 1633.

The composition of this book includes select recollections about several memorable relatives I have known personally. I have also read in many libraries about the lives of other New Englanders, many of whom are somehow related. Where extremely relevant, their stories are communicated in this remembrance as authentically as can be told.

The storyline presented follows the history of a few notable pioneers, including those who bravely and resolutely moved inward to the geographic center, or heartland, of the country under specific duress and great danger to survival. It returns again and again to the New England home, even if the wayward ancestors themselves never could (or chose not to). It frequently reaches back in time a few hundred years or more for the purpose of making realistic comparisons, and it even purports to educate our children and grandchildren, hoping to influence forever, in some way, presently undetermined progress for immeasurable times to come.

This writing project could be nothing but, at the very least, an abidingly whimsical or quirky history within the mere threads of a universal theme. It is an updated prologue, although a partial one, to contrast rare human progress with innumerable worldly concerns. At its best, it is an intimately intuitive and intensely observational piece about significant challenges and changes to the earliest immigrant community in America—in particular, one such family, taken to the natural results of their resources and abilities over the centuries leading to Ulysses S. Grant. Our story begins almost four hundred years ago, and it ends, solely for my own narrowing and increasingly limited experiences and purposes, now, about thirteen generations later.

CHAPTER 4

Fortuity

Genesis of Independence, Connecticut Connections,

Taking Unorthodox Liberties, and Fortunes and Misfortunes

IN THE GENERAL AMERICAN FAMILY progression, of course, millions of individuals have traveled and labored all across the land to build the nation as it exists now. Look around you. America is predictably less distant from perfection than it was just yesterday because it is, with rare exceptions, continuously improving. The Union has dealt with diversity through an ongoing structural means, the US Constitution, which embodies our supremacy over previous struggles and the collective wisdom produced from contemporary and ancient societies over millennia.

This development didn't take many thousands of years as it did in the rest of the world. The United States became a revolutionary worldwide power in less than 150 years. It is impossible to grasp the scope of the collective journey without the apposite perspective and insight found in books about Americans and in other treasured places like museums and national parks.

Survivors aimed at going long in life are mostly, like me, healthy, fit, and fortunate, and we would be justified in telling you that this once-future period of American life, extending from the end of World War II to now—my lifetime—has been a reasonably propitious time to be alive. My uncle Earl Hudson Grant survived battles in Europe during World War II and on the Korean peninsula during the Korean War. Fortunately, he married, raised two daughters, and lived a gratifying life into his eighties.

Of course, for many individuals, this simply has not been the case. For instance, I was named Thomas in memory of mother's eighteen-year-old brother, who died a soldier on June 8, 1944, in Normandy, France. As a family, the Youngs had migrated to Connecticut from Wyoming County, Pennsylvania, before the United States entered the Second World War. After selling the family farm, they had looked for non-farm jobs during the prewar defense buildup that was booming in Connecticut. Our grandfather believed and trusted then president Franklin Delano Roosevelt when he said that the United States was supporting the efforts of Western countries like England and France to defeat German aggression but was not entering the war directly. Both grandparents took jobs on the Pratt & Whitney Aircraft Company assembly line and were credited by other Pennsylvania families and relations for enabling their emigration to Connecticut also.

Despite the intense sadness and despair that Uncle Tom's death and the loss of friends aroused in that small vulnerable family, the Young household, I know that my birth a year later meant quite the sharp opposite, to the relief of my mother and my maternal grandparents, Louise James and Thomas Young. As soon as I was old enough to hit and catch a hard ball and to show some genuine appreciation, Uncle Tom's leather baseball glove suddenly appeared and was presented to me with a ton of family love and joy.

There was already a precise "pocket" firmly formed in this not-so-dated sporting surprise. It was said that uncle Tommy had liked baseball, and the story was confirmed by the impression in this glove—he had spent many hours as a boy tossing a ball fast and hard from his right hand to the glove in the left to create a neat, tight fit for that perfect and precise hardball shape. I felt inspired to do the same thing for many years in order to preserve, in my time, that fine old leather mitt and to demonstrate my appreciation of it to everyone. I felt a signature, serendipitous cognition that I was somehow connected to him: his memory, his love, his dreams, and his courage, and that somehow I was truly destined to fulfill my uncle's lost presence later in life, and then some.

The Grant family that Ulysses called "fully American" in his 1885 literary tour de force and autobiography, originated from the auspicious seventeenth-century marriage of an uncommonly daring young couple on the sixteenth of November, 1625, in Yorkshire County, England. The church service authoritatively recognized and approved this new husband and wife, uniting the inseparable futures of Priscilla Grey and Mathew Grant.

The wide-ranging significance of this particular marriage was not lost on Ulysses S. Grant six generations from then: he begins his own memoirs with what he knew about theirs and shines a spotlight on the grand emblematic significance of this historical unification for all descendants like him, the countless generations of European kin who were so represented in that most seminal family moment.

The couple had some socially audacious and confidential plans that could have invited persecution for unorthodox Protestant convictions if their desire for certain freedoms had been prematurely revealed. They surely faced the dangers of shunning and imprisonment in the event of discovery. They also knew that the specific odyssey they had chosen would seal their fate away from everyone they had ever known and trusted. Mathew and Priscilla prayed that it would become acceptable to their progressive families, and even to the whole world in the years to come, to put their trust only in God.

If you've ever been to the English coast in March, you can readily imagine the early morning gathering and departure. Chilling wind drove irregularly and powerfully in grimly anticipated blasts across the waterfront dockyard as it pulled sundry levels of darkening, semitransparent clouds mixed with the early fog swiftly away to the north. An imminent acquaintance, Reverend John Wareham, sporadically greeted and warmly offered his first long-expected salutations to all his fellow migrants. Within the hour he comforted the laid-back and chary congregation of the Puritan sect with the sanctity of scripture and an all-too-familiar prayer. Wareham spoke first of the prospect of a demanding journey that would deliver them to a new environment where they would be confronted daily with an utterly difficult but optimistically sublime and previously unknown liberty. They and the children would, each and every one, soon be free to make a personal covenant of worship and purposeful service, all in harmony with spiritual renewal through purity of thought, values, and deeds in a community of faith, charity, and respect in the new England.

After these words of hope, everybody joined the deferential Warham by reciting in unison a universally memorized prayer:

Our father in heaven, hallowed be your name. Your kingdom come, and will be done on earth as it is in heaven. Give us this day our bread, and forgive our trespasses, as we forgive those who trespass against us. Lead us from temptation and deliver us from evil, for yours is the kingdom and the power and the glory forever.

The new gathering responded with an unusually robust and emotionally charged "Amen," and they arose from their knees to resume cheerful introductions. As the sun also rose, the warmth began to lighten spirits, and Mathew and Priscilla bid their affectionate good-byes to parents, brothers, sisters, and local ecclesiastical figures before joining the others on board ship. As the mood generally became weighty and focused on the trip again, they now looked for a suitable place on the vessel *Mary and John*. This ship, in all its quintessence, departed port later that morning, the 29th. At sea a total of sixty-two days, the faithful began each day with Holy Scripture, a hopeful message, and their prayer.

Passengers from the *Mary and John* departed the ship at Nantasket Point (now the Dorchester section of Boston, Massachusetts). They carried a small practical assortment of European treasures with them. The Grants' only daughter, Priscilla (1626–69), had been born in West Country, England, less than a year after the couple's wedding. Now a toddler, she carried a doll her loving grandmother Alice had sewn together from remnants of cloth stuffed with straw shreds. Her parents carried only a few essential spiritual and physical belongings. On shore, the living remnants of the community that joyfully welcomed them now had been initially established no more than five years before in the Bay Colony.

The voyage of the ship *Mary and John* was the second to a settlement of tradesmen and planters that Reverend John White of Dorchester, England, had spent most of the preceding years meticulously planning. All forms of relief that homeland resources would bring to the village were enthusiastically welcomed. With this in mind, the Dorset minister had carefully recruited particular passengers and families, with much thought given to a viable and smartly balanced community of freedmen, servant apprentices, and planters from southwest Wales, the beloved country shires of Somerset, Dorset, and Devon, and the towns of Dorchester, Bridport, Crewkerne, and Exeter.

After the good ship securely set anchor, the Grants hustled, along with other passengers, to exit the newly blessed seaworthy ship *Mary and John*. Safe at last, at the end of the voyage, passengers felt intense emotions now. They were all very committed to an adventuresome fresh beginning. They viewed the new land through filters of enchantment, faith, and fascination. Each one-way passenger was tormented nonetheless by the anxiety of having left behind highly valued family relationships and extended community connections from their ancient towns and traditions. Their faith and dependence on each other would fill this unhappy void.

Two relatives were travelers of notable support and consolation: Thomas Grant, the older half brother of Mathew by a little less than a year, who would permanently settle inland in Massachusetts, and the two boys' sister Jane, who would migrate to the Connecticut River valley with Mathew and Priscilla. Of these two siblings, Aunt Jane remained closest to the family until she passed on gracefully at the very respectable age of eighty-five in 1690.

John Grant (1573–1640) and wife Alice De D'Urbervilles (in English: Turberville, 1577–1640) were both older than fifty when their children embarked from Port Plymouth on the *Mary and John* in 1630. They could not seriously think of doing likewise, abandoning the due comforts of aging peacefully at home. Even though their poor culturally persecuted hearts may have sailed in sympathy with their children, they were considered by everyone else too frail to make the tough trip to America and get any benefit overall from the opportunity.

These compassionate and resourceful Welsh parents fervently believed, as did the younger generation, in a principle of freedom to venerate God in a manner consistent with a properly prepared and continually devoted conscience. An atmosphere of threatening discrimination generated by official English orthodoxy had forcefully come between them and their own unyielding religious practices. Holy Scripture, congregational consensus, and a covenant of community service were the significant resources that ruled godly practices for them. In God they trusted, but certainly not in a king who enforced alienating forms of worship. Over the next ten years, patrician personages would not dissuade large numbers of religious men and women from joining a growing cultural movement that was first seen there in Plymouth by the dutiful Puritans John and Alice Grant.

Actually, the king of England and his cabal of grandee officers would come to prefer that those who persisted in challenging the absolute authority of the Crown's religion in the British Isles go to any place that seemed remote and permanently removed from Europe, such as the American colonies. Growth of trade with the colonies was a primary concern for a desirable norm of living, as it had always been between England with the cultivated world. The interests of the empire and the colonies further diverged, with separatists and loyal Englishmen alike being treated with continuing contempt and exploitation by the monarch's harsh narcissistic rule—so went the thinking of political-minded people like John and his philosophically inspired, professionally educated, venturesome, and promising son, Mathew.

It so happened that the River Indians of Quenticut (Connecticut) were faced with similar struggles in dealing with the tyrannical rule of the strong and powerful on the American side of the Atlantic Ocean. By 1631, Quenticut River tribes, including representatives of the Podunk, Scantic, and Tunxis Indians, peacefully visited and counseled the leaders of both parishes in Plymouth and Dorchester to resettle in Quenticut River Valley.

Quenticut River Indians Proposing Alliances

These tribes sought to create for themselves a more favorable balance of power and to prevent aggression from historical enemies. Several River Indian tribes had traditionally refused to join the confederacy of powerful North American Indians and were being intermittently strong-armed by warlike tribes of Iroquois, Mohawk, and Pequot. The local Podunk, Tunxis, and Scantic villages along the Connecticut and Farmington rivers were sporadically forced to pay tribute to enemies to maintain their independence. Even if ransom and tributes were paid, the unaffiliated tribes were often bullied, enslaved, or even murdered by insidious hostile hunting parties.

From Plymouth Plantation, an expedition sailed up the Connecticut River and assembled a small trading post structure but soon abandoned it all that winter, late in 1633. No further settlement was attempted until 1634 to support any claim to the property "near the junction of two rivers, north of Dutch Point." It was said that the Pilgrims sailed again up the Connecticut River, returning a little before an overland exploratory party of Puritans arrived from Dorchester in the spring. Mathew Grant and four other Puritan leaders were in this Dorchester group.

It soon became distressingly apparent that the Quenticut tribes had unknowingly brought sudden suffering on themselves even as they sought the protection of the friendly English from Native American foes. By the time the foreign planters brought alien armaments determined on settlement and alliances with the friendly tribes, they found great tracts of land prepared for planting but inexplicably abandoned. The fertile vistas were vacant due to highly transmittable diseases like smallpox. Sudden illness quickly reduced local Indian populations by as much as 90 percent. Unlike the inhabitants of Europe, the Native Americans had not developed natural immunity to these diseases. Unbeknownst to the European arrivals, long-dormant diseases had been inadvertently and cataclysmically imported to the New World peoples, who were almost completely vulnerable. This tragic quirk of fate seemed unusually sinister, since the Indians who had reached out initially, in good faith, to gain more security and a higher standard of living through trade with the English brought back little but appalling illness, misery, and horrible death for all of their commendable endeavors. This helped set up a murderous climate for aggressive colonial hostilities against the Pequot Indian nation, hostilities which continued to threaten the feasibility and longevity of peaceful settlement until a united group of colonial towns and Indians ended the threat once and for all by force in the Pequot War of 1637.

Podunk and Scantic Indians all but completely vanished from the area, with harassment continuing by aggressive enemies. Initially, Englishmen and their families were welcomed, but it was not long under these circumstances before the remaining Indian leaders sold great parcels of their land to the Dorchester men and migrated elsewhere. Now that the Great Migration from England had begun, many Native Americans who had the means and no continued appetite for growing demands to accommodate the foreign laws and customs of the English moved to the frontiers of New York, where they had more ancient ancestry and living kin.

From the first day of the arrival of the good ship *Mary and John* to the first anniversary of this transatlantic deliverance, Mathew had already fully paid the debt he owed for the family journey to America. A free man, he focused on achieving professional acumen and persistent enterprise to support the budding American Grant family. Delightfully, a youthful and industrious wife, Priscilla, safely delivered three more children after arriving in the new land. Her practical husband enjoyed helping care for the children but was otherwise profitably occupied as surveyor with a group of vigorous Dorchester parish community leaders who were planning an exploratory trip to the Connecticut River Valley to check on it for possible settlement.

The five Dorchester men in this group were gone for several months in early 1633 as they explored their way along time-engraved Indian trading trails to a fertile valley that was already copiously well known by the native peoples as quality hunting ground with rich sandy loam for easy planting. The trip itself was more than a 250-mile source of considerable hardship by foot that lasted no less than two full weeks overland. After duplicating their journey home, the men spoke enthusiastically of the region, as though it were just what the pastor had ordered, "God willing," for the renewed community parish covenant.

Along with the personal courage and inherent risk belonging to their new enterprise, each settler was given the gift of the "two-acre parcel of land." Mathew was instrumental in planning and giving these endowments at Windsor, as well as in the professional affirmation of which were the most utilitarian or defensible of the properties he had surveyed and mapped for the common good. He recorded all lots and deeds for every willing settler.

Bay Colony migration to Connecticut, circa 1633–34

Mathew Grant was at the head of a uniquely successful game plan because he had already effectively selected, mapped, and distributed family lots that would allow Dorchester people to establish a home and community of the godly there. By the spring of 1635, the families of these five West Country English explorers and their good friends had traveled together over and through wilderness from the northeastern coastal town of Dorchester, Massachusetts, to a new permanent home further inland and westward. They eventually called their second settlement Windsor, out of fervent sentiment for the town of their venerable homeland.

Mathew Grant's continued leadership in the parish community was devoted to the perfect egalitarian community. He expressed this devotion in the carefully chronicled church and official town clerk records that were his responsibility to maintain for more than thirty-five years: "I have never acted on the sole basis of the desires of any one man."

Signing as a witness, Mathew described one of the first archetypal land grants provided by the Podunk Indians that gave east-side river land away to the Puritan farmers for a favor and the uncertain vision of maintaining English patronage. Cultural similarities and vulnerabilities of both the local Indians and the Puritans established a mutually profitable status quo that seemingly benefited both ways of life for the time being.

Indians also put themselves in peril in this way: their indigenous customs saw private ownership as an incredibly alien notion. According to their traditions, the earth belonged to all living beings. The English made distinctions like whole class privileges, individual profit, and prosperity that followed many aspects of culture from the cradle to the grave. Propitiously, the interests of both sides created some years of room for peaceful agreement, but land grants always worked to the favor of New England in the long run.

The first land grant witnessed by Mathew specified that: "a Chief named Coggerynosset" (of Poquonock) testified that the land on the east side of the Great River, which had long been admired by Dorchester and Plymouth settlers, was Nassacowen's land, and that Nassacowen was so thankful about the coming of the English that he gave it all to them "for some small matter." Since neither party really understood what private ownership of land meant to the other, the first foreign settlers could purchase and own all the land they wanted for little more than promises. Of course, to Puritans, one's word was considered a sacred bond, as an Englishman named William Shakespeare had written in his play *The Merchant of Venice*, foreshadowing a generation earlier the gist of these surprisingly rakish English land deals.

Windsor, Hartford, and Wethersfield formed the colony of Connecticut in 1636, with the seat of the General Court of Connecticut in Hartford. The Fundamental Orders of 1639 established the principle that "the foundation of authority is laid in the free consent of the people." This was the first constitution in New England and has provided Connecticut with the honorable recognition as the "Constitution State"; Connecticut was the first colony to adopt a constitution in matters of self-governance.

Subsequently, all English settlements in Connecticut Colony accelerated development quickly, benefiting from peaking political unrest in the English Isles and a sudden explosion of the historic Great Migration from England. People left England in overwhelming numbers over the next several years until the exodus began slowing in 1640, but not before making it impossible for the Dutch to continue any viable claim to Dutch Point, Hartford, or in any matters that put them squarely at odds with the colony of Connecticut.

The youthful, hardy, and travel-willing families that originally journeyed overland to find a new home were certainly more than a little daring. Though fearful, superstitious, and cautious concerning mysterious and unfamiliar creatures in the backwoods, both real and imagined, they pushed on along the sacrosanct journey westward until they located the "promised rough country" of no prior rules or restrictions that was so incredibly desired. These forebears were so energetic, and so supernaturally inspired, as to walk all the nearly impossible wilderness way, step by devoted step, in order to secure the previously denied settlement of all inbuilt liberties and freedoms.

At the old Windsor village green today, visitors will find an aging and pretty much indiscernible bronze plaque dedicated specifically to the godly couple Mathew and Priscilla Grant. The memorial is positioned toward the front of the original lot where the loving couple maintained their first permanent home. Located in a nook at the edge of Main

Street, adjoining the old town green, it is all that now remains visible of the Grants. One can still imagine their second American-born son Tahan Grant's blacksmith stable adjacent to and just south of this in the village green, along with other necessary businesses like the barbershop, near the narrow pathway to the palisade. Across Main Street, about two thousand yards away, is the First Congregational Church building that became an iconic prototype of nineteenth-century church architecture for parishes in Connecticut. Indoors, the Windsor Historical Society displays Mathew Grant's original surveying equipment, as well as the detailed map he drew up for the original village. The Society is supported and maintained by local citizens and family donations from those who have freely migrated all over the state, New England, and the nation at large.

Heather Grant, May 1985

Under the auspices of the Grants, Windsor became the first community settlement in Connecticut, with Wethersfield and Hartford not far behind. Puritan pioneers finally reached, developed, and practiced their well-conceived and gracious philosophical style of living in a new, more suitable place than they had ever lived prior to this achievement. Here along the rivers were wide plateaus and long plains that would be used to engender a newly sanctified and abundant American family life.

In principle and practice, the Puritan settlers found it necessary to create an entirely new existence remote from the officially dominated government, or politically sanctioned church of their homeland, and even from that of their first Pilgrim neighbors in Massachusetts. The newcomers were disappointed that the privileged men of an aristocratic elite already ruled their Massachusetts parish. To this day in Connecticut and throughout the country as well, Americans enjoy a division between religious orthodoxy and state laws like that first developed in Connecticut by these evenhanded and inclusive Puritans.

The conscientious early legal independence of church and state rule guaranteed the American civil rights and responsibilities of personal choice, democracy, religion, security, and justice, without unfair discrimination, to all the people. Those decent citizens who are educated about the importance of these distinctive early social conventions do not underestimate, or take for granted, the virtually supernatural agreement of our forbearers, an inspiration that made America an enduring worldwide beacon of indivisible freedom.

CHAPTER 5

The Great River Valley

Second-Generation Americans, East Windsor Hill,
"Windsor Farmes," Three River Plateaus, Early Professional Careers,
Occupations, and Trades, Colonial-Era Military Conflicts, and
The First American Patriots

THE FIRSTBORN SON OF MATHEW and Priscilla's embryonic American family was Samuel (1631–1718). He grew to adulthood in Windsor and learned surveying and carpentry from his father and by assisting men of the first generation in building America's primary colonial structures, many of which last to this day, nearly four hundred years later. Young Samuel operated the river ferry between Windsor and the fertile land directly across the Great River that was being used only for secondary agricultural interests in the beginning. After several years, he was the first in family to build a home on the third river plateau at East Windsor Hill. This third and highest river plain was where builders of the second generation made their homes if they were in a fortunate enough position to do so. A lofty location on Main Street signified prestige, but among the more socially ascendant and mobility-minded citizens, building on the third river plain was practical for keeping residences of the newest parish above the high waterline during annual spring flooding along the Great River. Samuel was the original robust, hardworking, culturally esteemed, and commendable progenitor of the eighteenth president's family bloodline, as represented in its seventh generation by Ulysses S. Grant.

The second son, Tahan (1634–93), became the forbearer of the family branch to which two brothers and I belong as samples of the Grant family's twelfth generation. Samuel and Tahan were the first generation descended from Mathew and Priscilla Grant at the brotherly bifurcation of two long, direct, and interesting genetic paths.

I do not follow all children of the original family in this particular research, but have met members of the Humphrey and Anderson families at a contemporary conference of the Descendants of Ancient Windsor held in Windsor, who were very excited and pleased to be related to the Grants through firstborn daughter, Priscilla.

Research would certainly be in order to determine whether or not John, the last-born surviving child of Mathew and Priscilla, became a progenitor of family descendants like Samuel and Tahan. There are some recently obtained indicators that suggest John Grant (1642–84) and descendants helped settle the towns of Simsbury, in Hartford County, Connecticut, and also Torrington and Litchfield in Litchfield County. John married Mary Hull in 1660, and the couple had as many as ten children in the twenty-four years of their marriage. I have heard that John may have had only two surviving children. If this is ever substantiated by research, our Samuel and Tahan relations will have played a much larger role in the settlement of western Connecticut, where I now live, than I have discovered to date.

John is acknowledged as a leader in battles against the Native Indians in King Phillip's War (1675-1678). Since almost every house was burned to the ground in their battles, Simsbury had to be rebuilt almost entirely after the war. This was eight years before John's death, and so he and his brothers would have a hand in this early reconstruction effort.

Samuel and Tahan, are the brothers followed intently in this record. These two brothers opened distinctly different paths of life almost from their births. Samuel inclined toward a generally worldly approach, demonstrating social- and civic-mindedness in his time. At eighteen, he was industrious and totally in charge of the first river ferry between Windsor and East Windsor. Several years later, he was one of the first of his generation to build a small full-time residence at East Windsor Hill. As an adult, he built and ran a cider mill and became part owner of the first sawmill among River Valley communities. He would become the leader of local enterprise and parish developments, much like his father, Mathew, but he was distinctly more secular and involved in daily work. He became wealthy through a diversity of well-coordinated interests and initiatives that were well suited to his physical strength.

A primarily artisanal interest animated Tahan. He set up his first shop on the Windsor village green. As a young man, he was drawn to the physical jobs at the stable in the village center, and he applied his considerable physical strength to neighbors' commercial and residential material needs as their first blacksmith. He was content that the practical tools he brought into being through his control of wood, fire, and iron, combined with his physical strength and sense of aesthetics, would reliably benefit everyone he served in the village. Tahan's business acquaintances were the ubiquitous down-to-earth local farmers and tradesmen who possessed markedly fewer worldly expectations for a formal education. The second son married Hannah Palmer at Windsor on January 22, 1663. The couple rented and resided on the Michael Try lot near the Palisado until Tahan, following Samuel, became one of the first petitioners to migrate permanently across the river from Windsor to develop the new community parish of East Windsor, in May 1680.

Tahan was the second of the family to migrate to East Windsor and build, but he made his farm on large open acres deeper east into the highest plateau, a mile or two from Samuel's farm. His brother's property extended from Main Street to the river, sloping sharply to a second elevation and then descending again, extending even lower for a little over a half mile on the first planting plateau, all the way to the riverbank. These three plateaus, with their new houses and the most fertile sections of the parish, were all together called "Windsor Farmes."

Technically, Tahan's farm was developed in the "Wapping" section of East Windsor. It is likely that the locale was named for a street in England that was well known by that name. Wapping is also one of the names of a section of Wales that holds historical connections to the Grant family.

Samuel Grant, Jr., (1659–1710) grew up in East Windsor, becoming a farmer and a carpenter by trade, like his father. New parishes of Wapping and South Windsor were established through his many projects, as well as those of others of the second and third generations. As they had sons of their own, brothers Samuel, Sr., and Tahan, Sr., worked simultaneously with several companies of builders and sold lumber and hardware alongside their sons and daughters. Many newcomers built all along Main Street, along the whole length of the high plateau, as other towns like East Windsor developed.

Tahan, Jr., (1665–93) married Hannah Bissell, uncle Samuel's East Windsor Hill neighbor's daughter, in 1690, at the age of twenty-five. This couple had just two children together, a daughter and son. The son, Thomas was born on October 1, 1692. He was not to have the satisfaction of knowing his father Tahan, Jr., well, since the man died in April of the following year, at only twenty-eight years of age, in an accident at his uncle Sam's sawmill. Due to the father's sudden absence, the family fell into the habit of calling Thomas, "Junior."

Thomas (1692–1769) grew up on the Wapping farm with his mother Hannah, his sister, and paternal grandmother, Hannah Palmer. First cousins Noah and Thomas ("Junior) naturally became very close companions, since they had played and mastered the construction trades together from infancy to adulthood. They both grew up to be competent carpenters and painters under the tutelage of Samuel Grant, Sr., and Noah's father, Samuel, Jr.

On July 9, 1722, Thom married Elizabeth Rockwell, and the couple lived at the Tahan farm, to which Thom's late father Tahan, Jr., had made several additions, with assistance from uncle Samuel, Sr., and Tahan, Sr., years before the sawmill accident.

Known for many years as a talented tanner, shoemaker and leather-goods merchant, Thomas also served his colony as a captain of the local militia, which engaged in battles against English enemies during King George's War, and the following Indian Wars between 1754 and 1763. Thomas earned a commission as a lieutenant, still fighting and training local boys in the militia as an elder. His cousins, John Grant Jr., of East Windsor, and Captain Noah Delano Grant, Jr., of Tolland, were fellow veterans of these conflicts, which involved French nationals from Quebec in a murderous alliance with the hostile Mohawk Indians.

Last, but certainly not least, Sarah Grant, the daughter of Tahan, Sr., married into the Ellsworth family and gave birth to son David Ellsworth in 1709. Subsequently, on April 29, 1745, she became the ancestor of the future Honorable Oliver Ellsworth. Oliver served as the first chief justice of the US Supreme Court after following the Revolutionary War. An extremely unpretentious, practical, and frugal man, Oliver refused his carriage and rode a horse to the Continental Congress in Philadelphia to help write the new

Constitution of the United States. He rode his horse from Windsor, Connecticut, to Philadelphia, Pennsylvania, and back home—all the while, no doubt, drafting and redrafting thoughts about liberty, justice, and the self-government of free men in his reasonable and respectable mind.

Megan Grant, May 1985

CHAPTER 6

Genesis

Travel, Trade, and Family Deoxyribonucleic Acid (DNA):
Continental Europe, Ireland, Wales, and Scotland

HOWARD LESLIE GRANT, JR., WAS the first to tell me, "Actions speak louder than words." Father was a man of prominent action, and he had a sharp, pointed, informative aphorism for every subject. This characteristic seemed intended to resolutely secure his unquestionable authority, and it served to end any meaningful dialogue with a child. I did not ask him too many questions, but strangely enough it has come to bother me that I never did ask him about his middle name. It could have been a family name, but only from a very distant, still-unknown great grandparent. When visiting Ireland in 2014, I found that the name was still renowned among some old manors, churches, and castles of the ancient culture there.

The common denominators of Grant family DNA are likely aspirant, adventuresome, prosperous, and culturally proud ancient Celtic peoples from Western Europe and the first-century Roman conquests from the Mediterranean along the Iberian Peninsula to the Irish Sea between Ireland and Wales (West County England); from the north, our ancestors include the plundering Viking (Norse) warriors and later

Norman Knights from the eleventh to thirteenth centuries. The most predominant characteristics include a promising and pertinent purpose, unspoken stratagem, self-effacing wit, and if unduly put down, put off, or taken for granted, a tendency toward shunning or prevarication but never an openly scornful, snarky narrow-mindedness with fetid language in public. This said, I admit that such propriety is ideal and seldom completely lived up to consistently, with the exception perhaps of a few saints or family prodigies. An even more perfect and morally mature person could also demonstrate forgiveness of any intended, or unintended insult, and avoid further scornfulness or display of anger. A pure character maintaining this exceptional standard would be difficult to approach a second or third time without contrition, or with any resemblance remaining of the former insensitivity, prejudice, or inappropriate audacity, when their personal fault had become apparent to all.

DNA test results from the spring of 2014 confirm family anecdotes that was passed along from generation to generation by word of mouth and ultimately reached me. No doubt that if Ulysses Grant took the same tests today, the results would be familiar. Long before the 1600s, DNA had been pulled up the line of Grant men, our ancestral predecessors, by the works of the consistent male Y chromosome. While the predominant results affirmed an ancient ascent from western European peoples, a percentage or two of the results were indicative of Roman and Iberian family relationships also.

The supposition that Grants came to England with William the Conqueror, the Duke of Normandy, in 1066 is one hypothesis. Corroborating evidence would need to be found to provide historical support for this idea. The first records of the Grant surname in Scotland date to 1258, with the appointment of brothers Laurence and Robert Le Graunt as sheriffs of Inverness.

Family likely immigrated to Scotland after the Norman Conquest and subsequent rule, which included ruthless taxation and repression of subjects in Scotland, Ireland, and Wales. The custom of surname use became common in the English language of the Isles in this specific historical developmental period. The Normans were great builders and were responsible for constructing many of the large, awe-inspiring castle strongholds, cathedrals, and warehouses from the profits of taxation during their significant empire building and international trade.

The Grants of Scotland held the highlands in the Strathspey and Loch Ness regions, paid taxes due the government, and customarily followed the leadership of the many powerful English monarchs, but devotion to the king and royal family became fractious over religious creeds and the issue of free expression.

Grantown-On-The-Spey is a highland rural community along the Spey River that has existed for centuries. In early spring 2015, we visited there briefly with a van tour around the entire circumference of Scotland. Grantown was robust, with various family activities on a Saturday afternoon in the town center, very much like those any mid-size town in the United States might have today. In particular, we saw a village fair with booths selling homemade goods and several practical artisanal creations.

Our ancestors became well situated as gentry and commoners in Ireland, Wales, and Scotland—at somewhat different times, perhaps, but within the relatively brief epoch of perhaps a century or two. Quality of life progresses regularly, and great strides can be made in four to eight generations. In England itself, a previously well-known region nicknamed "Grantland" existed in what would later become contiguous sections of both Lincolnshire and Warwickshire counties.

At Wormleighton, in Warwickshire County, England, William Graunt of Grantland (1439–79) married the Lady Graunt, "Heiress of Grantland," three years his junior. Apparently, a son, William E. Grant (1479–1550), and descendants were born in York. His male descendants included John (1504–93), George (1534–96), and our Mathew's father, John (1573–1640).

Mathew's parents were unknown to researchers of the Grant family, including me, until the difficulties of performing international genealogical research from faraway places like Connecticut were eliminated by the fortunate availability of the World Wide Web. I report here, for what I believe is the first time, that the ancestors of our Mathew of New England were living in southwestern England (Wales) and north as far as York, within the powerful influence of London, at least five centuries, or twenty generations, before reaching America in 1630.

Middle Ages documents show that people who took the Norman name of Le Graunte initially inhabited southern Ireland. The Le Graunte family of Waterford, Ireland, was related to Milo Fitz David, a Norman knight and son of David Fitz Gerald, Bishop of Saint David's Church, which was located just on the coast of the Irish channel in southwest Wales. In 1176, this influential knight, Fitz David, was granted one hundred thousand acres and received the title Baron of Overk, in South Kilkenny, Ireland. His son David Fitz Milo Le Graunte ("Le Graunte" meaning "the strong") succeeded him and was the first in this family to permanently use the surname Graunte.

Baron and wealthy landholder Milo Graunte generously gifted the Augustinian nunnery of Saint Mary at Kilculliheen and left it well endowed from his riches. By the late fifteenth century, the ancestors of the Graunts of south Ireland and Wales were wealthy merchants in trade with Spain, Portugal, and continental Europe. Waterford City records show them moving from their home at Kilkenny in 1500 to Waterford. Thomas Grant became bailiff of Waterford City in 1542, and in 1546, James Grant followed as bailiff in the years of 1549, 1557, and 1560.

With the Internet, we can learn something new or different almost every day. In the lack of any evidence to the contrary, we may find synchronicity in the truth that many families united behind the name Grant over the centuries. The name was a good name meaning "great" or "strong," and this "family" has indisputably migrated from all over the world in times long before recorded history and since, as momentous will and wealth would allow. Since it was traditional in Europe to keep the land intact for the eldest male heir, a large number of sons and daughters could find more amenable individual opportunities only by traveling far from their childhood homes.

CHAPTER 7

Coherence

Heritable, Individual, and Social Similarities or Differences,
Agronomic Society to Industrial Work

FAILURE TO ASK LIVING RELATIVES about family, about our historical
roots and cultural heritages, is a failure of lucidity. The poor preparation
of our children and inadequate acquaintance with these facts, is linked
to limited contact from one generation to the other. In particular, I
experienced this related to the mysterious family name "Leslie" since it
appeared as a strange anomaly that both father and grandfather shared
the name, and nothing was ever discussed about it to the children. I
have thought that the answer would show up in family research sooner
or later, but absolutely nothing has come to light. Thankfully, of course,
I've learned so much more than heretofore expected from research. All
aspects of family history seem important now.

Howard Leslie Grant, Sr., died suddenly one late afternoon from a
heart attack in 1959. This happened only a few months after his retirement at the age of sixty-nine. I was not quite thirteen years of age then.

This unfortunate event was more or less precisely what the US
government considered would happen to most retirees when it crafted
Social Security for retired elder Americans in 1930. Work your whole

life, pay taxes for Social Security, and in your feeble years die within months of collecting your entitlement.

In the early part of the twentieth century, the average male life expectancy was sixty-five years. In this regard, sadly, grandfather was not the fortunate exception to the official expectations.

Due to difficult labor conditions throughout American history, many years of longevity were far from a sure thing for the workingman after his retirement. It was almost so in my father's retirement years, but he lived to be eighty-four. His generation was only the beginning of remarkable advances for the treatment and prevention of cardiovascular disease. The successes in prevention of heart and other diseases, along with the rise in longevity these successes have sponsored, multiplied rapidly in contemporary times. Fatality in adulthood, more often than not, steel seems rampant among those who reject a physician's advice for lifestyle changes beyond age sixty-five. Increasingly, the survivors are not random lucky ones, as in father's time, but those who are able to make difficult choices to eliminate all health risks such as torpor, depression, cigarette smoking, liquor drinking, and prolonged use of unnecessary drugs. Many forms of addictive behavior, such as eating too much, eating too little, or consuming lots of the wrong foods for one's maximum neurological and biological well-being, were increasingly common over the last four or more decades.

Granddad's death happened early in the year, just before spring turnover, or nature's transformation and natural rejuvenation. In his time, Howard walked everywhere and obtained enough exercise, but his diet may have been compromised, wrongheaded, and deficient much of his life. Obtaining a well-balanced diet with sufficient amounts of certain essential nutrients like protein would have been a serious predicament for people during the two world wars and the Great Depression of 1929, all of which Granddad survived.

Robert had just turned seven years old a couple months earlier, and we were left alone for the first time while our parents took our baby brother, Steven, and left us for much of that evening to be with our grandmother in Manchester. Mother's parents arrived a little later, so we were not alone long. Our maternal grandparents lived about six miles away, at 733 Griswold Street in Glastonbury.

Our Grant grandparents lived on the rented side of a split two-story house at 117 Summit Street in Manchester. Since our ancestors had left the family farm in Wapping, it had taken our direct family connections about three generations until Father and his brother Earl could make a satisfactory down payment on the purchase of family properties to avoid rents for housing.

The hospital was only a block or two away, but Grandpa died at his home, as many others did back then. There were few efficient and effective hospital services offered, and it was problematic to leave the security and comforts of home for any sudden aches or pains. The major symptoms of diseases were known, but emergency medical care wasn't as readily available. A family doctor still made comforting house calls but could do little more without the support of the broad range of medical procedures available at hospitals now.

Granddad had worked several non-farm industrial jobs to make a living and support the family in his lifetime, including shoveling coal into blast furnaces as a foreman for the local international soap manufacturing plant in the north end of Manchester. Coal was the typical heating fuel then. Coal bins were located in dark cellars that had light only from small windows in the daytime. This made the battery-powered flashlight a grand innovation for manufacturing, assembly, and sales to every home after its invention in 1889. When the coal was delivered to homes by industrial wagons, and later on trucks, a ton of coal created an unbelievable racket as the solid material slid down a wooden chute and through the window to the coal bin down under. Though I only heard coal discharged to the basement this way one time, I'll never forget the loud racket it made.

At thirty-two years of age, Mother had just received a driver's license and was itching for some free time, so she left Robert and me at our grandfather and grandmother's place on the day we heard the noisy delivery of coal. We were visiting on a perfect summer's day and played in the area between homes shared with the next-door neighbor's kids. It being a weekday, Grandmother watched us while Granddad was at work.

She was very accommodating and gave us lemonade and her customary homemade banana bread. It really wasn't so bad, even though I remember not liking it very much then. Many years later, long after Grandmother passed, I developed a taste for and appreciation of banana bread largely because of my fondness for recalling her thoughtful efforts, years before, to please me. Nice children, even today, would never intentionally hurt a grandmother's feelings. So I remember lying very carefully and consistently about really liking banana bread. Despite my good intentions, I felt very guilty about lying to my grandmother. She kept asking me the same question every time we visited, and I lied again and again! We visited her what seemed like many more times, and we were always offered more banana bread. No matter how badly I hated her banana bread, I would always cover up the unspeakable truth with dreadful lies. Now, of course, it's doubtful that she ever actually believed me, but it's too late to find out.

Mother had her driver's license, and that meant a lot to her. She felt fortunate and more independent as an adult woman for the first time ever since her marriage. She was able to do so much more for the family on her own than had ever been possible in the past. Still, I missed the togetherness of going grocery shopping with Dad and Mom as a family on Friday evenings. Now, the less restricted Helen Grant would go shopping alone on weekdays while we attended school. The upside to all this innovation was that we got into the enjoyable habit of watching television together on Friday evenings. In comparison to the modern young women of the 1950s, our grandmothers never bothered to get licenses to drive the family cars and would take the bus to go anywhere their husbands did not also go. Granddad's mother, Emogene, walked everywhere, or was carried there by a horse and wagon, because automobiles were not mass-produced until 1914. Although the women's suffrage movement ended in 1920 when women were guaranteed the right to vote, the overall culture was still stubbornly resistant to change in many ways. Motor vehicles were available only to the rich, who could have one custom built by local engineers and mechanics at hardware stores in New Britain and Hartford as early as 1903—the average man had to go without or share the family car with other licensed motorcar drivers in the house.

When Granddad's grandmother, Mariah Dunham, had to give up the 1670 Tahan Grant family farm in East Windsor, she left in a horse-drawn wagon with three grown children, including Josephine, Louis, and his wife, Emogene, with all the family belongings that might be needed in the city. According to Uncle Corwin, they were poor, but his father Louis didn't sell the farm until convinced to do so by his brother-in-law. They did not leave Rye Street, Wapping, until then. The old bi-level colonial at 22 Pine Hill Road, Manchester, became their home as Granddad turned sixteen years old and Corwin was still just a kid. Corwin reflected on this family life-altering event understatedly: "Farm work was for other folks since then."

The Manchester residence had already been converted to a two-family house for renting to people who were making a transition from farms to the city for non-farm jobs around the turn of the century. This first residence in the city looked pretty much the same about the time I remember meeting Uncle Corwin there for the first time. Corwin never married. He prevaricated by explaining that his mother had poor eyesight due to glaucoma and he could never leave her alone for a long time. He was—sadly, I thought—very much alone when we visited the old family residence a week before Christmas in 1951.

My father and I huddled together, as close as we could get to warmth from a hardly heated wood stove in the living room. We stayed less than an hour, but it seemed much longer due to the cold. I remember looking repeatedly at Dad, expecting to hear an excuse to leave and go home, but he obviously had much more in common with Uncle Corwin than I knew about on that occasion.

I recall how cold it was but also how familiarly we were greeted and how affectionately we were treated by this stranger. This was the first time I felt a discernible inquisitiveness and sympathy or empathy toward extended family. My uncle was so obviously pleased to have visitors. Everything about the visit made me feel self-conscious and unexpectedly inadequate socially, especially when we left, as we probably did, a bit too soon. It was certain that my uncle had nothing he could think of to make us dally there with him a little longer.

Dad and I never outwardly acknowledged the cold, the inadequacy of the stove, or our inability to relate comfortably to Corwin. My father did tell me that Uncle Corwin was the only relation he could remember needing family charity. He said, "We needed to pass the hat around one time to help him." I asked, "What does that mean?" but he let the details drop there.

Grandfather's brother Corwin was just a nice guy with a generous disposition, a working man with little income who cared deeply for family and specifically for his elderly mother, who was "a little too old for company" and remained in her bedroom resting during our visit.

During the entire time we visited that day, my great-grandmother's path and mine could have touched briefly. But her bedroom wall would separate us forever. This lady was Emogene Hudson. She died in 1951, only days after this visit.

At some time on another visit, I remember Corwin telling us that his grandfather was "a very nasty man." I discovered that Norman Owen Grant (1831–1900), our great-grandfather, had been born in Wapping on the 1670 Grant family farm and had married the fourteen-year-old Mariah Dunham of Mansfield in the month of July 1855. It was quite unusual for a young woman of fourteen to get married even then, but Norman was the son of Wyllys Grant (1793–1855), a farmer who had married Norman's mother Emily Hosmer. Since Wyllys had died at sixty-two years of age, the selfish twenty-four-year-old Norman needed a wife to help him and his mother Emily around the large farm. Norman didn't know anything pertaining to his contemporary midwestern cousin Ulysses S. Grant, and if he had, he would have wanted nothing to do with the clouds of social unrest from that territory. Norman could be counted on to tolerate Southern ways because of his own need for help around the godforsaken and bothersome farm he had inherited from Wyllys. Like many in Connecticut at the time, he was aloof and demeaning on the subject of Federal issues. Likewise, Ulysses certainly didn't know of our second great-grandfather, Norman, and that was not something N. O. Grant would have wanted anyhow.

"Nasty Norman," as he was called in the Manchester family circle much later, was blamed for the only shameful divorce in a proud family's history and for abandoning the farm life on Rye Street and his family. According to Corwin, his grandmother Mariah was the "sweetest and kindest woman that there could be, or ever was." As a boy, he had been delighted to spend time with her, he recalled.

Non-farm work in Manchester, Grant's Market, circa 1908

In Corwin's words, "we were poor" because his grandfather left his grandmother Mariah and the farm. The two fatherless children left behind included Louis Dunham Grant (1859–1934) and his younger sister, Corwin's aunt Josephine. They had little, if any, means of pecuniary support, being left as they were at an early age, and this led to great suffering for the family. Generations earlier, men and women had often married a second time because of the higher mortality rate and the greater chance of becoming a widow or widower. Uncle Corwin's father and Jo matured there under different and very difficult circumstances.

The move to Manchester was pretty much an act of desperation and accommodation to societal changes. My great-grandfather Louis soon became the local butcher, using skills he had perfected by working on the Grant farm. As a young man, he assisted his uncle Wilber F. Grant in setting up and managing the People's Market in the north end of town within a half mile of the rented Pine Hill Street house.

Until his death at seventy-five, Louis was a night watchman at the Cheney Fabric Mills. He was lucky to have any job in his senior years to pay the rent. Other members of the family were employed in the family drugstore and food market for sundry jobs. Ostensibly, even Louis's children regularly assumed roles in the shop for aspects of their livelihoods from time to time. One of these young people was Howard Leslie Grant, Corwin's brother and our grandfather, who was a vigorously healthy young clerk of about seventeen years of age then. I believe he is the thin, fair-haired young man on the store-front steps in the picture of Grant's Market that is reproduced above. I say this because Dad and I looked almost identical to this man at that same age and definitely not so much like others who may or may not be distant relatives. Howard, Jr., was eighteen in 1939, so the lad in this picture must be his father, since the absence of cars and trucks and the presence of a horse and wagon suggest that the entire scene took place in the beginning of the twentieth century.

Although not exceptionally tall or particularly big and muscular, the Grant men began adulthood very lean and sturdy, like the young man in this picture. They made good employees, and due to their quick performance and high potential, they sought and found leadership roles that more than satisfactorily employed their unlimited aspiration and ambition. These young men were undaunted by temporary setbacks and showed little emotion or disappointment, remaining resolute and brave under duress. This American brand was focused, dependable, and devoted, particularly, in extraordinary work, through which they aimed to improve their personal standing and recognition in the community. Their character tended toward egalitarian principles that enabled them to be more empathic, understanding, and less patrician then many equally intellectually endowed but socially and emotionally exclusive peers.

Physically, their heads were large to extra large, and longer and narrower appearing than those of many other Europeans. Nearly half the head, including the chin, mouth, nose, eyes, and eyebrows, made up a tad more or less than one half of their faces—the rest was forehead and cranium, which could make possible the normally favorable impression of larger-than-adequate brain size, and maybe even better-than-assumed functioning, too. But arms, legs, and fingers, were all a bit too short for straightforward excellence in performance physically in most team sports, let alone to allow them to take success for granted, achieve less stress from casual repose, or easily achieve, and maintain any dominance in competitive athletics. The only exception its possible to think of is the well-known example of Ulysses Grant, who was superior in horseback riding, particularly at West Point, New York in the 1840s.

Howard Jr. recalls that in 1931, Grandfather walked southward on Summit Street, past the North End Elementary School, on the way home during lunch hour every day. One aspect of granddad's job then was to pull the chain on the Bon Ami soap factory's steam whistle exactly at twelve o'clock. Since the whole town of Manchester adjusted its pocket watches and daily routines at lunchtime by this loud, resonating steam whistle, granddad must have proven a reliable, steady, hardworking, and trusted man, just like his own father Louis before him.

During the lunch hour, granddad would leave the factory for exactly sixty minutes and briskly walk past the school, eat the lunch prepared at home by grandmother, and return to work to be the initiator of the factory steam signal once again, calling employees to recommence working throughout the factory and in the industrial

community. He was happy being responsible and reliable and receiving recognition for his work. Most times, he walked home for
lunch as he was, completely blackened from coal dust head to toe as
the result of loading shovelfuls of coal into the blast furnaces that
powered the enterprise. Due to his socially amenable disposition, he
was fondly given a nickname, "Happy Howard." His smiling face
and wide-open eyes as he waved toward the school were the only
features father could recall as being clearly distinguishable on that
coal-blackened face and body.

My grandmother Rebecca lived on granddad's Social Security income payments to the age of seventy-nine. Even though I knew her
for longer than I knew my grandfather, I—to my regret—failed to dis-
cuss the Leslie family name with her, though she did tell me that her
maiden name was Noble and great-grandmother Grant's family name
was Hudson. Emogene Hudson married Louis on June 1, 1885. My
great-grandmother Emogene's parents were Esther Williams and Cyrus
Hudson, as I learned from my research at another time.

Hudson Street was only a city block from Pine Street. Perhaps
Emogene first met my great-grandfather Louis on that street after moving from Somers, Connecticut, where she was born. Grandma Grant
once stated, "Hudson was your great-grandmother Grant's name, like
the explorer Henry Hudson." I always thought she meant to tell me outright that we were related to the Dutch explorer of distant Long Island
Sound and the Hudson River Valley.

Thomas Noble and his wife, Isabella (Bella) Crockett, emigrated
from Ireland and Scotland at the beginning of the twentieth century, in
1903. Grandma was a little girl when they left northern Ireland to work
and master woolen manufacturing in Scotland. After learning to be a
wet-velvet finisher, he brought his family to America and went to work
at that job in the Cheney Fabric Mills in Manchester.

I passionately wish I had asked more questions about all of this family history to document their memories, and I can't imagine not thinking about our family history more often and more deeply as a child. Of course, people didn't have the means to easily research family history then. Public libraries were few and far between, and people in the city often needed to walk to get anywhere. So parents and grandparents may have also been more than a little embarrassed not to know more detailed answers about their own heritages, especially for the anticipated shallow examination of a child. Sadly, too few words were focused on things important to the future, or to the past, in those days.

The normal range of their daily activity extended only a couple miles from home at best. Unlike their predecessors three centuries before, they could even walk to church services and back home again on a Sunday morning. In the city of Manchester, in the 1900s, there was a big Congregational church on Main Street (in the North End) and a large Methodist stone church (in the South End) whose size gave one the impression that they more than adequately served those important congregations.

The Grant fathers bore the paternal signature Y chromosome and the norm of "holding back" inescapably well. One might even think nothing really wonderful, exciting, or delightful had ever happened to them serendipitously, or that no such unintended and unexpected events were considered worth talking about. One could even leave their company essentially feeling undervalued, misunderstood, and unappreciated, as if one had told a joke that went over like a lead balloon in the wrong company, but the men were also uncommonly physically and socially perceptive, aware of surroundings, informed of propriety and appropriate spheres of influence, coolly unassuming, and usually nonjudgmental, logical, considerate, and tacitly restrained about choices of free will in life on earth. Certainly they did not dream of their own fame or tower high above the authentic world. Once my father told me critically, "If you can't say something nice, say nothing at all." This being said, our father was an adept listener, unexpressive in important but typical family matters, a taciturn, impenetrable, and mysteriously silent man.

CHAPTER 8

Countenance

Intuitive Thinking, Research Methodology,
Selective Service, Proctors of Peace, and
Self-Determination

BY EXAMINING INTRIGUING FAMILY STORIES, genealogical hints, and widely read research, I have confirmed that Ulysses Grant's American heritage and mine actually began with that same marvelous cohort, Mathew and Priscilla Grant and family. The couple gave birth to and successfully parented at least two surviving children, who became progenitors of their own distinct and direct Grant-family American branches. This detail, plus all the surnames incorporated into family genealogy over the four hundred years considered, means that many thousands of American citizens, if not tens of thousands by now, share this great union with the Grant family in America.

Compared with many buried and obscured cousins we will never know a great deal about, Ulysses S. Grant is indeed unique, well documented, and of specific interest to the world. For the simple sake of comparison, consider the fact that our twelfth generation was born a very eventful one and a quarter centuries after, or six generations removed from, that of U. S. Grant. Family ancestral records do substantiate that the eighteenth president of the United States is a particularly blessed, virtuous, honorable, and glorious sixth cousin. This hallowed fact has been very difficult to grasp even over a lifetime, let alone now, with the requisite humility.

Ancestry.com indicates that Ulysses S. Grant is a sixth cousin four times removed. I might simply take their word for it, but I believe that he is, as a matter of fact, only three times removed because of the technical implication of our birth order. The third child born to the Mathew Grant family, and the second born in America, was Tahan Grant, the ancestor who was a family branch patriarch of mine and the first brother of Samuel Grant, the president's forefather. A third son, John, was the actual fourth sibling, and his direct descendants are presently generally unknown. Incidentally, President Grant's direct hereditary line has been obscured for at least three recent generations by information marked "private." So in order to know more, we must wait until the Grants directly related to Ulysses and Julia make information about themselves more widely available.

At any rate, it is almost certain that trifling technicalities of birth order are really important to almost no one, and yet this example is a convenient illustration of the fact that we should not accept at face value everything that's written as final truth, no matter what the platform, since more can always be learned and examined in a different light. There's also the obligation to point out, in a valid contradictory sense, that no matter the exact order and span of time that have passed between us, rational denial and skepticism are important for scientific methods to be adequately employed in any required research. As familiar likenesses emerge, they must be proved valid or invalid through painstaking research methodology and rigorous professional standards. Or so I thought, perhaps somewhat obsessively. The drive to continually doubt personal research results was perturbing, but I suppose the mystery being incrementally resolved, as it eventually was, became more spiritually meaningful and intellectually inspiring as more of the truth was uncovered and became known beyond any understandable doubt.

New knowledge about Ulysses and other relatives was always exciting but remained somehow also extraordinarily deniable, even unbelievable. I continued living my own separate but not totally detached existence for many years until retirement. I gathered all my evidence tentatively until it was possible to fit together the separate known pieces of accumulating evidence with total rational accord.

Curious hints of similarity involving supposed appearance, temperament, and idiosyncratic behaviors typically disturbed me because coincidences appeared to belie the notion that Ulysses was not related to me (a null hypothesis) in a significant way. It appeared many times that one could argue for an even closer biological relationship if it were not for the century and a quarter that had undeniably slipped silently between us as if we were old ships in the night. For instance, very much like his immediate sons, my brothers and I resembled Ulysses in some clearly memorable ways. I pointedly recall the first few times I really studied President Grant's image on the fifty-dollar bill or examined a photo by Matthew Brady of Ulysses in the Civil War, wondering why he resembled my grandfather and father or even my brothers so much. As these questions filtered through my conscious thoughts, it was almost inconceivable to me that I had had no true awareness of history prior to the event of my own eye opener. How could I have not assimilated in some way the awareness of a great civil war, two world wars, the Great Depression, and the like? It was always really inconceivable that all these great events had actually happened before me, but—not in a small way—also to me. So my interest in kindred spirits was endemic throughout my own early years of experience. This was years before research validated the family ties that had always been readily verifiable, though only to those who could remember, or who could imagine all possible results and use investigative historical tools to accurately observe the past and make acceptable inferences and deductions about extended family.

Throughout my childhood, long before our common heritage was tested or confirmed, I reasoned and marveled, in random sophistry and naive thinking, that perhaps I could have been divinely engineered and also uniquely predestined for contributions to a greatly celebrated cause. Coincidentally, so it seemed, due specifically to President Grant, I imagined that some great human potential penetrated or mutated our family bloodline and would someday reveal itself dispassionately somehow, indicating that I was living not only a provocative but also a crucial and decisive destiny. Thoughts that a vital personal providence would come about any number of years along a narrow continuum of a simple faith, revealing to me my preordained purpose, were calming. But self-perceived imperative signs, like any based solely on a personal point of view and supported by inappropriate methodology, failed to prove individually, or collectively, permanently affirmative or satisfying, even though I examined them time and again.

As I gravitated to certain career changes, there was a predisposition that I think was vainly nurture. I felt it was natural to take on difficult leadership responsibilities. Put another way, it was impossible, a real blind spot, to think of any leadership challenges that would end up too difficult, be unsatisfying, or work out badly for me. It seemed necessary to accept even the most impossible endeavors. If others were not chosen for a challenging position, then that position came to seem, of course, as some supernatural gift that I would gladly accept like a qualified servant, or like an envoy extraordinaire.

Awareness of my ideas and sensitivities was in all ways seemingly natural, intuitive, instructive, and ascribed by a divine grant or by an all-knowing entity. I was not absolutely certain, but I was more than willing and expectant to assume some clearly noble, patently self-sacrificing, even profitless occupation that promised to develop exquisitely inspired leadership potential and yield the most positive results. I remember that, having managed somehow to earn a doctoral degree by the age of twenty-one, I thought that just about anything was absolutely possible from that point on.

The motivation to physically document personal life experiences, like those within his memoirs, came to Ulysses Grant late in his life. Ulysses said that he had nothing imperative to add to what so many others had written about. He always underestimated the importance and cool clarity of his writing and even dismissed as unimportant the acute damage of despicable lies that others could write about him with impunity. It was hardly enough, but Ulysses would not recognize these people by name in public again. He even consistently procrastinated over writing his personal memoirs until he was facing his complete and certain obliteration, not from critics but from a rapidly advancing final battle with throat cancer. Finally, Grant was sufficiently motivated to put his personal thoughts in writing. A compelling arrangement with a trusted friend, Samuel Clemens, who would act as publisher of the memoirs, and the guarantee of a favorable financial future for the former president's family clinched the deal.

So in comparison, I would surely have no abiding story late in retirement such as his to inspire and instruct the future generations. But like him, I reasoned further that continued procrastination could be unjustifiable behavior. Undervaluing the story I knew and could tell, even casually allowing for my own customary laid-back manner, would certainly lead to significant sadness and eventual despondency in my elder years. But having a true book in my hands would always lead me to satisfaction: I would always have at least one meaningful item that I had created and crafted over time. By personally respecting the superlative historical importance of Ulysses Grant's writing, I wanted to fearlessly and quietly eschew trivial matters for a change and readily follow his fine final example.

Alternatively, all this may have begun when I read a book titled *'Twixt Twelve and Twenty*, authored by the 1960s singer Pat Boone, that my maternal grandmother had gifted me for my twelfth birthday. From reading this book came my first thoughts about talents and what would constitute unique individuality. Through a process of exploration, experience, discovery, and validation, I intuitively investigated what could possibly become of sparks of energy and enlightenment in the existent course of reality through a space and time that I represented. Maybe, after all, I would in time truly embrace a project and be remembered because of this one, or the other, if nothing else.

Could one even leave any coherent and comprehensible legacy? If so, what would historically be that small but ultimately meaningful fragment of purposeful space and time? What would it proclaim about intentions and direction in a once very small and painfully atypical case of transmutation?

For God's sake—after all was actually said and done, and seemingly regardless of truth and honesty, everybody seemed to perceive the well-known Ulysses S. Grant differently, one in not-so-civil disagreement with the other. That led to more questions: "What is actually reality? What is the simple truth? If anything, what is truly authentic and lasting?"

The disparager could dismiss all pensive past expectations for authentic recognition as an irregular series of chronically reoccurring and sadly out-of-reach daydreams, full of positive intentions but also excessive youthful self-importance and delusion. What I wrestled with, or really conscientiously worried over for many years, as it appears now, was a personal philosophy of living, which underwent continual construction and reconstruction and would in the end intently encompass all the discoverable universal laws of nature in general, and of my nature in particular. I came to believe that my purpose was to live a long, productive life and leave a significant number of quality contributions that would speak to my sincere devotion to truth. Of course, it's ironic that good intentions so often lead to so much angst and self-deprecation, for recognition of intended great victories is typically so elusive.

Admittedly, I weighed every new experience for its relevance to a probable heroic global career path that would be dependent on good judgment, adequate available runway, adaptive skills, and even tons of old-fashioned good luck. This complex artist's palette of potential responsibilities and commensurate risks and rewards apparently rested on the false assumption of a linearly absorbing integrity and the bequest of a peculiarly determined DNA to guide my sagacity looking forward. The big question was, "Will I ever make the smallest steps and the most confident choices aimed toward an ultimately meaningful future?"

The outset of the notions related to a disquieting individual characteristic like this made me ever more anxious and restless for a laudable personal purpose and a corresponding authoritative knowledge base. What rational moral being could knowingly waste the supposed single true chance given of leading a principled, meaningful, and purposeful life? Certainly not me, if I could figure out what preordained purpose or fate was actually waiting, dormant and readily available, to spring to life in my soul, spirit, mind, and heart. In summary, I sought always to do the right thing, at the right time, for all the right reasons. This was a reliable and tested procedure I employed to discover my true grit, or the intended course of my earthly journey. In the end, significant results would prove whether or not I had perceived the proper career path and adhered to it correctly. The not-so-consciously planned but most positive and significant outcome of my internal striving was a keen mindfulness of worthy moral values.

In grossly unfitting contrast to all the above, I was blindsided by the first letter I received as certified mail from the federal government of the United States of America. All boys were directed to register for Selective Service at "their local Draft Board" after their sixteenth birthdays. Until that letter arrived just before April 30, 1962, at the parsonage of the North Haven Methodist Church, or my home, I didn't even know that I personally had a local draft board! What a disappointment.

When I turned eighteen in 1964, I received another certified letter instructing me to take a physical examination for induction into the army. Unlike many of those in the two long parallel lines of completely naked boys and army physicians in New Haven, I passed the physical and was "A-OK" for conscription.

I couldn't claim an exemption fast enough as a conscientious objector. Fortunately, the Society of Friends offered counseling services for prospective COs in Hartford, and off campus, at Storrs. I attended meetings at those places with counselors who I thought had been COs long before me. These men were, in fact, only from the generation directly before me. I began to perceive the transparent dots of reality, connect them, and see that every generation throughout all of time was fraught with other people's causes. It is a fact that somehow these external causes are made to look like one's own unique purpose for being. That's why only boys were drafted and the so-called cause was unlikely to withstand the test of time in the long run. Sure enough, in the span of a lifetime, we would become the friends, rather than the enemies, of Vietnam. If this war was personal, though, only God could know what I would have actually considered doing under different circumstances.

I believed in an epiphany that had come to me in church, as all big ideas did in those days. I argued, "Would it not be immoral, and unconscionable on religious grounds, to let anyone instruct me to kill others?" Yes, I believed it immoral to kill another and immoral still further to blame a scapegoat for my success or failure. How could anyone possibly put another person in that uncertain situation for any purpose?

This was my first existential crisis! Someone else could claim homosexuality or commit dishonorable crimes and go to prison to get an exemption. You eventually heard of all kinds of culturally sanctioned loopholes, even rumors about boys intentionally cutting off fingers and toes to avoid the draft. It was called Selective Service because only the best physical and moral specimens were selected to dispute with death and killing, the government's concerns.

Fortunately, I had some very good counseling from the Society of Friends, and I had two Methodist clergymen, including Dad and Reverend Fran Carlson of the First Methodist Church of Hartford, to stand up to the draft board and to vouch for the authenticity and sincerity of my convictions on religious grounds.

My personal aim from 1965 to 1972 was to be selfish and stay alive to continue higher education and to be prepared to fully live later for a noble cause, rather than to lose control of my individual conscience and die for someone else's aims. There was no acceptable argument for involving young boys in a civil war in Vietnam that would be acceptable in the eyes of God, I thought. And as surely as there is a god to determine my own way of thinking, I was correct.

While I remained diligent and steadfast on this issue, my intellectual focus became increasingly more reliable and predictable in terms of its future usefulness for reflection and discovery. I wondered often what my ancestors had done in similar circumstances. From the heightened sensibilities of childhood to the educated discoveries of a mature historical-minded analyst emerged a genuine metacognitive awareness and deeper appreciation for the simple grandness of the single life's incredible potential. Coincidentally, my independent brand of person had been reinforced time and again by successful discoveries as my understanding of the Grant family steadily improved.

One of Ulysses Grant's recollections was initially inspiring to me in particular. Even he had wanted nothing to do with the military in his youth. However, he did want to obtain the best education available. Ulysses liked subjects that he could easily learn on his own, like mathematics, natural sciences, and artistic expression through drawing and oil painting. He made quick study of these subjects by naturally doing well in the classroom. He also had an affinity for novels, which may have helped stimulate interest and imagination for the great big romantic picture of personal self-determination.

His father simply announced that Ulysses would be going to the US Military Academy for a college education. He became eligible after another young man from their hometown suddenly dropped out after only a year at the academy. When the senatorial nomination became available, Ulysses's politically mindful and sufficiently connected father, Jesse, knew the local congressional representative well enough to ask for the nomination of his eldest son for the exclusively available, all-expenses-paid educational opportunity. The boy disliked even the thought of a military career but could not deny that he could get the best education available for himself there. He thought that he would leave the army after graduation, after any obligation was paid, and teach college-level mathematics or geography as a graduate from West Point.

Likewise, overall, I too cared to do moral, meaningful work and be worthy of love and admiration like other respected family members. A career that was to be personally satisfying and rewarding and provide opportunity for continual lifelong education, like that of leadership in some applied profession, was ultimately as attractive to me as it had been to Ulysses.

To impress them, I also remember audaciously promising a few close relatives like my father that I would experience life and a career as an adult and then write an informative book about life and our family. No one ever discouraged this impulse to reach further into the past and into the future than they had done, or even expressed a caution pertaining to a propensity for overreach that was obviously evolving and being intensely nurtured by a forward-looking boy in their midst. Nor did anyone point out the overwhelming likelihood of failure in such an unnecessary, self-imposed, multifaceted, and open-ended responsibility.

But that was a long time ago. I was young still and uncompromisingly unrealistic and as confident in ultimate worldwide triumph and prominence as one could possibly be when facing the ever-expanding and often overwhelming world. Despite vigorous persistence, the whole world is much larger and greater than one can really understand at eighteen years of age. At least it was then.

In the end, everyone can do something, just not everything. Knowing this truism, one can make it a priority to concentrate on actions that yield the most good. Becoming a conscientious parent, for example, is a superlative achievement that makes many other things possible.

Hannah, the assiduous mother of Ulysses Grant, was a homemaker. She exhibited steady habits and seldom left the house unless it was to go to the local Methodist sanctuary for sustenance and spiritual renewal. Neighbors reported seeing her sweeping the porch almost every afternoon but rarely otherwise encountered her outside. Hannah never made the trip to Washington, DC, to visit the White House even when her son was elected president of the United States. But Ulysses recalled that his mother had never spoken an unkind word about anyone. She lived a considerate, devoted life and raised a gracious and enlightened son.

CHAPTER 9

Second Generations

Settlement of Land Grants, Colonists Transformed,
Walking In The Family Footsteps, Three Patriots Named Noah

ON THE FIFTEENTH OF MAY 1673, the General Court of Connecticut in Hartford pronounced, "This Court grants unto Matthew Grant of Windsor one hundred acres of land without the east bounds of Windsor." Within a year, our Mathew reassigned this land grant to his eldest son, Samuel, who had ambitious plans to build houses with resources from his sawmill and help from Sam, Jr., as part of the general development of the colony's Tolland County. Junior's son Noah and at least one cousin, Thomas Grant, were enlisted to work on building the new houses as carpenter's apprentices. The boys helped the elders strategically choose lots at the pinnacle of a long, thickly forested hill almost equidistant between the two new nascent towns of Coventry and Tolland. This land grant became known among local residents in both parishes as Grant Hill. The well-traveled single gravel path between the two towns, up and over this gentle five-mile-long hill, was called Grant Hill Road, and it is still referred to that way today.

Noah readily took the first of the indulgently and carefully constructed houses as his own for the raising and grazing of animals and general farming. Thomas helped build the second colonial house next door under the astute supervision of Samuel, Jr., who pretty well became this youngster's father also after the sawmill accident that took the life of Tahan, Jr., only one year after Thom's birth. The boy's grandfather Tahan, Sr., was also sadly absent from Thom's entire family life, having died at the age of fifty-nine later the same year, 1693.

Samuel Grant, Sr., maintained primary propinquity to Mathew Grant by maintaining residence in East Windsor and would control the strings of family ties to the seats of influence in Windsor and East Windsor. Of course, all the benefits due to community patriarchs like Mathew Grant gradually changed and became diffused among the sons and even grandchildren like Samuel, Jr., Noah, and Thomas as these young men found parish horizons expanding and vying for the attention of the second and third generations.

Much like his grandfather in Windsor, Noah was inspired to grow with a new parish along with his own farm. He took as his responsibility, though, remote acres of rough land to clear of forests and fieldstone. There were no fields all ready for plowing left for him by the Indians. He found and fell for a beautiful and peaceful location with great views by which one could see over the tops of trees for miles to the east. Even now, you can see the eight-miles-distant lights of the University of Connecticut, a land grant university, on a dark, clear, and starry night.

Noah's land offered much in the way of fieldstone for walls and wood to burn for cooking and heating but significantly little soil ready for profitable farming. As though Noah did not actually have enough to be disappointed about, his partner and cousin Thomas was needed at home by his mother and sister in Wapping on the farm he had inherited from Tahan, Jr. Thomas couldn't be in both places at any of the many times he desperately desired to be to please all his kin.

To Noah Grant his isolation and the loss of inclusion in his synergistic partnership with cousin Tahan, was only the beginning of dire and downright depressing consequences. The life of Noah, third generation presidential forbearer, would not again intersect with the republic in fewer than four grating generations. The next generations of the president's ancestry were to illuminate dramatically all truth in the axiom "When the going gets tough, the tough get going."

Many years of heavy work continued to take its protracted toll on the third-generation pioneer farmer in Tolland. As fortune was panned out for the family, cousins were stretched apart by diversity of opportunities in different directions. Another oldest son, Noah Jr., was more than willing to help his father as needed as he gradually he came of age, but he still had several years to go to reach full potential as a farmer when the overburdened thirty-three-year-old Noah died in Tolland.

The idealistic young son, Noah Delano Grant, along with his brother Solomon, became caught up in significant historical events leading to full-time military service in an early, and for them, an even perhaps premature call to arms. Both sons were full of patriotism, and Noah even exhibited a propitious talent for leadership when war with the insurgent French and Native Indians became the new patriotic cause of their era. It was during this eventful time, a year or two later, that Tolland would send a groundswell of colonists to the New York Colony war zone. In 1757, Tolland and towns in the vicinity quickly raised an army of several thousand men to an alarm that had been raised by patriots like Noah and Solomon, who warned that French and Indians were on the march to attack the English colonial Fort William Henry.

The venturesome Grant boys had sought to do something with their lives, to do something for their families and country beyond anonymous rural farming, and so the brave brothers fought with the British army at a couple of remote outposts in the New York colony. Noah used his physical skills as a carpenter to rebuild one dilapidated fort on the frontier during the first year of his service. A year later, he further distinguished himself by leading colonists and Great Britain's Rangers on patrols of the land and remote settlements, which had been under growing active attack by the French from their base of harassment on the Canadian side of the Great Lakes. Unfortunately, by 1756, as the war dramatically escalated and recruitment alarms resounded, both brothers were reported missing and considered dead after they failed to return from a scouting party in the vast, enemy-infested wilderness.

At the news of their loss, sentiment in Connecticut began to grow that the hometown hero Captain Noah Delano Grant could have become a great American general in the next war, but this sentiment took a back seat during the existing armed conflict, which lasted several more years until culminating in victory for the colonies and the British in 1763.

The battle-hardened colonial survivors were exceptionally hopeful for peace and prosperity for many years to come, but in just thirteen years the Yanks in Connecticut would find it necessary to form the Continental army. This army would be well trained and hardened by sacrifice, and it would turn resolutely against the British, the colonists' former proctors of war.

In the bicentennial year, 1976, I was unexpectedly startled by a written description honoring two heroic brothers, Captain Noah Delano Grant and Solomon Grant, soldiers from Connecticut, as my family and I visited Fort Ticonderoga, New York. Upon weighing the suddenly spine-tingling prospect that these two soldiers were quite possibly related directly to us, I researched their names to uncover more material about the family, particularly as it related to the direct phratry of the great Civil War general Ulysses S. Grant.

Five or six years later, as I was intently reading the 1981 work *Grant*, by William S. McFeely, I was motivated to aggressive research about how Ulysses Grant was influenced by his family. Mr. McFeely had made some questionable speculations and inferences about the bloodline of Ulysses Grant, perhaps only to stimulate, much to his credit, some acute researcher's response. He suggested that Ulysses Grant had not come from a distinguished family, as the renowned General Robert E. Lee of Virginia certainly did. The Southern general's father and grandfather were well-recognized military figures to scholars of American history before 1860, and the supposition appeared to be that Grant's military acumen was simply a fluke of fate that arose out of nowhere, was inherited from nobody, and as such could not be considered as honorable, worthy, and as validated as that of Lee.

The McFeely biography, being the first scholarly manuscript I had read about Grant, seemed sadly if not tragically flawed, even offensive to anyone related to the Grants, in my opinion. Even worse, no one else seemed to know or care about this book at that time.

A proper and powerful interpretation of the impact of the Grant family on the nature and nurture of the greatest patriot and American military officer of all time was devastatingly debased by obscurity. It even appeared that during my lifetime no one would care to acknowledge or examine the significance of this critical disregard for reality and reputation. Grant's qualities buried by systemic chauvinism, the resulting errors of omission cast doubt on a true American and his family.

The long list of the Grant family's patriots and its services to America was categorically unknown by respected scholars long before McFeely's Pulitzer Prize–winning book. While not as one-sided or critical as articles published in the early twentieth century by die-hard insurgents, the book had the effect of creating, apparently solely in me, an intense, righteous urge to respond to all pugilistic presumptions once and for all. I am thankful that this so-called objective and factual biography of Ulysses Grant instigated and energized my efforts to uncover unknown, relevant material that was still reachable from the depths of darkness, particularly from the momentous vantage point, at first unwittingly held, in the state of Connecticut.

Finally, the awe-inspiring trip to the colonial Fort Ticonderoga in upstate New York fortuitously directed my attention to and focused my awareness on significant military service by the Grants' colonial forefathers, even those who lived a century and a half before the Revolution.

Working from the memory of a small number of clues, and by carefully examining the life spans of the relevant kin, I effectively resolved a lingering mystery about General Grant's direct family lineage. I reasoned that there had existed not just two, but as I suspected three Noah Grants. This knowledge successfully joined Ulysses's father Jesse with a third Noah. This meant that Jesse was inherently linked to the two great-grandfathers of the same name, on direct to Samuel Grant, Jr., of East Windsor, Connecticut. So the fact that Ulysses's grandfather, and two great-grandfathers were all named Noah had the unintended consequence of averting many previous scholarly attempts to complete ancestral family links properly between U. S. Grant to our original path-determining Mathew and Priscilla Grant.

The president's line was very problematic and frustrating to decipher for those not related to President Grant or incredibly devoted to the truthful remembrance of him and his ancestry. I understood that the first Noah lived a short and difficult life of only thirty-three years. Then, Noah Delano Grant lived a brief one also—he lost his life as a noble and commendable captain in the military at the age of only thirty-eight. One could hastily conclude that both of these men were only one single man if one did not know the storied details of their lives or perhaps failed to examine dutifully the birth and death records of either one. The understandably questionable, distinct existence of the third Noah Grant, who continued the lonely and obscure work started by the two preceding great-grandfathers of the president in Tolland, Connecticut, is hard to imagine when one's reasoning is woefully unaided by truthful factual matter. The actual identity of the historic Grant family farm, in Tolland, which was ultimately inherited and sold by Jesse Grant, was obscured by misunderstanding of the adult lives of all three men and their closest of kin. When the virtually anonymous, thoroughly belittled, shunned, and punished, third Noah Grant of Tolland abandoned his home and farm in bankruptcy for the new adventure and the perceived personal advantages of moving from Connecticut westward, he was suddenly cast actually back in natural synchronicity with a promising family propensity, the renewal of a long journey to the wild and new frontier of the bright, shining, and tractable setting sun. He was unabashedly eager and momentously liberated from stiff prevailing prejudice, and discrimination against him back east. He was motivated to seek better prospects for nature's endowment of self-determined satisfactory endings. Though he died two years before his famous grandson's birth, the third Noah became Ulysses's number-one family hero, and the young man was absolutely certain that he knew well the *one and only* "Captain Noah Grant."

CHAPTER 10

Noah Grant

Migrant Father and Great-Grandfathers,
Unbelievable Big Yarns, and Scholarly Pursuit

Taken all together, the Grants were a quiet, unassuming, never proud, and hardworking if not at all an intellectually consumed bunch, but not every individual character was always so inclined. Each generation had certain family members somewhat more like Ulysses's grandfather, the third Noah.

Noah was notorious in close family circles for his passionately recollected stories about his father, the real Captain Noah Grant, and his fighting in the French and Indian War. As a young man, he heard much about this from veterans of the war that venerated his father, Captain Noah Grant. In turn, he was then perhaps treated unfairly with wry skepticism for embellishing tales of his own participation in the Revolutionary War that always seemed somehow very exaggerated to his peers.

Upon hearing about the first battles at Lexington and Concord, Noah passionately claimed to be one of the many authentic Americans who left their plows in the field and answered the call to arms against the powerful British Empire. Ulysses readily gained the generally appropriate impression that he was the expected courageous extension of a long family line of American patriots, bravely spirited men and women. His parents had even abandoned the long family tradition of naming offspring after apostles in the Bible in favor of naming him after the Greek warrior Ulysses, who had a marathon mystical journey on the way home from the Trojan War. Jesse Root, who preferred the name Hiram Ulysses, had no formal American military service but was a vociferous abolitionist and Union supporter, as well as the editor in chief of the local newspaper in Galena, Illinois.

Certainly Ulysses's grandfather, originating from Connecticut as he did, knew about other effulgent patriotic veterans, from the throng of provincial farmers to the few weighty and worldly liberally educated, and he would energetically tell anyone who would lend him a sow's ear in the West about his thoroughly American pedigree. The town of East Windsor, for example, formally enrolled more Grant family men to fight for independence (fifteen) than men from any of the many other families drawn to the American Revolution from there. This number of soldiers was nearly equaled only by two other families in the East Windsor community, the Allens and the Bissells.

The list of bona fide volunteers included Gustavus Grant (1759–1841), the grandson of Thomas Grant and the son of Mabel Loomis and Samuel Rockwell Grant (1726–96).

In direct comparison, Noah and Gustavus were sixth-generation cousins. But Noah himself was not on a list of East Windsor volunteers or on any other list that has been found in Connecticut. However, Noah did have a younger brother, Captain George Grant (1750–1820) that did serve boldly and consistently during the Revolution with a Connecticut company. George probably became the basis for some of the stories the third Noah told his children in vividly embellished detail decades after the Revolution. Noah gave everybody the impression that he had personally seen all the great battles of that war himself.

Two soldiers from the Wapping section of East Windsor, Gustavus's brothers Isaac and Elisha, were captured and held as prisoners for a year on HMS *Grosvenor*, that was anchored in New York Harbor during the war. These men suffered greatly but survived the tight quarters, filth, and perpetual darkness of a below-deck prison until Levi Allen, an East Windsor compatriot, somehow arranged for an unlikely parole for the two. The wily Isaac reenlisted after his release and once again successfully challenged the odds favoring his demise, during the winter of 1776–77 at Valley Forge with George Washington's army, before returning to his beloved Wapping East Windsor home and a victorious hero's welcome.

The third Noah Grant was so unfortunate as to end his Connecticut tenure in a debtor's prison, shamed and regrettably unable to pay his hardened old cantankerous Yankee farm creditors. Pitiably, there was no record kept to provide a pension for Noah's supposed military service, and by 1782, it was clear that officers and widows collected half pay for life from the state but Noah did not. This, of course, led to some understandable conjecture about Noah's actual role, if any, in the American Revolution.

Upon his release from debtor's prison in Connecticut, Noah migrated through Pennsylvania and Kentucky and then to Deerfield, Ohio. Starting a new family, with a young second wife whom he married along the way at the age of fifty-three, Noah gave the name Jesse Root to a newborn with the intention of honoring the Connecticut lawyer who had helped him through the dreadful Connecticut bankruptcy. That the attorney, Mr. Jesse Root, received any other form of remuneration for this valuable service is doubtful and invites further skepticism regarding Noah's efficacy. One can easily imagine Noah saying, "Though I hope to have the wherewithal to pay you some day for all your trouble, I'm certain to name any newborn son after you, Mr. Root."

Jesse Root Grant probably knew his father, Noah, about as well as or better than anyone, and at least on one occasion vehemently verbalized his criticism of the man as "lazy." But only favorable sentiments seemed to be assimilated by Noah's unselfish and uncomplaining grandson, Ulysses Grant.

Ulysses recalled in his memoirs that his grandmother was "a Miss Kelly." We know that she was Rachael Miller Kelly from Kentucky and that she gave Noah as many as eight additional children before predeceasing her husband by ten years in 1809.

Owing to Noah's continued poverty and the death of the heavenly Rachael, the children desperately needed relatives to live with, or to go to foster homes. Jesse Root, the oldest of these unfortunate children, went to live with the family of Judge Todd in Ohio, and shared family dinners with the judge, his wife, and various other very needy youngsters, including a sullen and quiet boy named John Brown. As an older teen, Jesse even worked on the Brown family farm and witnessed father and son's sharp tirades against slavery.

John Brown became infamous for leading an armed attack on the large Federal garrison at Harper's Ferry, West Virginia, with the objective of freeing all the slaves even before the Civil War had begun. Rarely, if ever, did Jesse Grant mention his acquaintance with Brown, but his famous son reflected on this bit of history. Ulysses was certain that Brown must have been crazed to think that he could free all enslaved people with so few men. John Brown was arrested and hanged along with all of the conspirators who had not been killed outright by soldiers in the battle at Harper's Ferry.

Jesse could not have known why it would be so important to provide his progeny with many details about the family, but Ulysses was always interested in his patriotic ancestors' roles in the birth of the nation. Ulysses knew that he had a straight line of great-grandparents.

He knew—this fact would become important later—that some of these loved, respected, and appreciated ancestors were named Samuel. He hadn't had the time or the tools to automatically sort through all the details of the lives of these ancestors, but the specific knowledge he did hold close in his mind and heart would lead to credulous and compelling insights and creative problem-solving in his honorable career.

A particular incident from the young man's education is revealing in retrospect. Due to father Jesse's resolve, rather than Ulysses's own individual inclinations, the adolescent reluctantly but respectfully committed to the plan to take his higher education at the newly established US Military Academy at West Point, New York. There, his awareness of family heroes would serve him from virtually the very first moment of his contact with the school. Without any family present, facing the registrar completely alone, Ulysses was immediately confronted by a situation that ominously threatened to disqualify him from beginning classes there. Concern about his identity suddenly emerged with the potential of disruptive and disturbing consequences.

Ulysses arrived at the Hudson River Valley campus after a long trip from the mid-west to officially register for classes, and he found that his congressional sponsor had listed his name, incorrectly, as Ulysses S. Grant. The congressman from his district had erroneously assumed that an *S* would suffice as the young man's given middle initial because Simpson was his mother's maiden name. There was immediate confusion, and the facts could not be readily examined, due mostly to the generally insufficient state of communication for resolving even the most minor mysteries in the nineteenth century. The acute concern in this instance was to correctly identify the individual who was trying to enroll as Hiram Ulysses Grant when surely no one by that name had been nominated.

No one could say what the senator had in mind when he recommended the young lad, so to satisfy the registrar, Ulysses accepted the name as written, Ulysses S., and previously unknown fellow students fortuitously seemed to settle the issue by demonstrating an immediate penchant toward nicknaming him Uncle Sam.

This nickname was readily entertained, if not enthusiastically embraced, by their new classmate because he knew that grandfathers, uncles, and even extended family cousins had been named Samuel, or Sam. Though entirely unexpected, the tribute of his future classmates resonated very well with him. Perhaps even more important, he had experienced several times before in school and the community how his real given initials quite piteously and predictably encouraged the not-so-apposite nickname of HUG, and he knew that this nickname would seriously hinder the development of a satisfactory reputation at the US Military Academy. He felt no enthusiasm for dealing with the resulting ridicule and sarcasm that could bedevil his every waking moment. The staunch and even auspicious name U. S. Grant proved acceptable enough to him and ultimately would to the US Army as well.

CHAPTER 11
Pertinacity

Inspiration and Industry, Parental Guidance,
High Potential, and Self-Actualization

IT WAS NOT UNTIL THE late 1960s and '70s that my two brothers and I broke with the traditional occupational inclinations of our Tahan Grant–connected kin and earned professional degrees from New England colleges and universities. A perfectionist writer and sermonizer, Howard Leslie Grant Jr., our Methodist clergyman dad graduated from Hillyer College at the University of Hartford in 1960. He was the very first known college graduate of our hereditary line since the very beginning with Samuel's Grant's brother, Tahan. To achieve his difficult scholarly and financial objectives, dad worked at successive full-time jobs as an aerospace tool designer and production manager while taking evening classes for eight years in his "spare time" for the bachelor-of-arts degree. He then worked as the pastor of the North Canton United Methodist Church, as well as of with a colonial-era church named to honor one of the founding fathers, the Washington Hill Methodist Church. Dad studied to get the redundant bachelor of sacred theology degree from the oldest American theological college, the Hartford Seminary Foundation, which had had its beginning in

East Windsor during Tahan and Samuel's time. Father capped off his lengthy formal schooling with a master of sacred theology degree from Yale while serving as the pastor of the United Methodist church on Clintonville Avenue, in North Haven.

The Washington Hill church assignment was an interesting one— to me, the most interesting one. Dad was required to only provide one service a year to that church, on Christmas Eve. He explained that it was still a sanctified church in the Boston Conference of the United Methodist Church even though there were no members who could, or would, contribute to its yearly operation. Local sentiment for the church ran very high, so the old sanctuary was open once a year for prayer, a sermon, hymns, and the traditional Methodist rituals. The property actually had no regular parishioners, no sexton, no water, no electricity, no heat, and no light. When this was explained, I readily accepted my mother's suggestion and helped Dad clean the old sanctuary that year. I remember lighting oil lamps and at least two dozen white candles for the windowsills and alter. I also lit a seemingly antediluvian wood stove, its enormous stovepipe running the entire length of that sanctuary, to generate a little more heat for that cold service on Christmas Eve. The service had an otherworldly, ghostlike appearance, given the circumstances. Come to think of it, I've never felt a closer bond to my father or devotion to life than on that ebony starlit night deep in the Connecticut woods. Finally, every one of the unexpected, offbeat souls who slowly wandered out of the dark and into the dimly lit church was a little stranger to me than felt comfortable. Each ephemeral presence appeared as the quintessence of a time long gone.

My brothers and I followed our father's educational pursuits in the decidedly secular professional domains of education, psychology, and law. If it had not been for my father, I could not have imagined being a student continuously from the time of public kindergarten instruction to my years studying for the highest university diploma given, the Ph.D. degree. I think the thought of losing momentum, or underperforming by interrupting my education, was threatening. I did not want to take the difficult route that Dad had chosen. Mother mentioned often that it is just too taxing on quality family life to be at school so long. She knew that I would want a better life for a wife and kids. In all regards, though, my father's chosen profession was supernaturally stimulating to our family.

Along with great potential comes great responsibility, and the Grants were certainly a living manifestation of the model of purpose, planning, persistence, and ultimate durability invoked by that axiom. The same must be said about Ulysses Grant. Ulysses was duly trusted with care of the family's best horse and wagon for assistance in his father's work. This trust was quickly earned and well deserved by the spring of 1834, as Ulysses entered adolescence. He experienced with his family the challenges of growing up in this country under the stress of trying to make good on the promise of America. Like all children born and raised in this land, he felt the pressure of the grave issues that are shared and transferred from a parent's generation to the next, issues that shape the formative daily conditions for the integrity of the republic and a democratic society. With tempers flaring on all sides of important national issues, tight lips and reticence were justifiable day by day.

In his memoirs, Ulysses affirms the importance of powerful human relationships in his family and credits many influential aspects of his boyhood experiences at the raw edge of early midwestern society. For instance, he recalls the angst he felt at the overwhelming sounds and sickening slaughter of the meat-processing activities across the road from his home, in his father's tanning factory. This early industry of his father physically and mentally disheartened Ulysses, and the boy wondered if he would ever escape a stigma he felt of technically being the frontier butcher's son. The otherwise normally healthy and dutiful young man promised his parents that he would do any chore asked of him without complaint, with the exception of working there, at that despised business that his father owned.

He kept his promises and aided his father's interests in another significant way, albeit as an uncompensated and unassisted supporter: delivering travelers and leather goods to Cincinnati, at least seventeen miles from the home and factory. At no older than fifteen, he began this work and apparently reveled in assuming total responsibility for the inherent challenges of managing horse and cargo on the trip from his frontier home in Georgetown, Clermont County, Ohio. Privately, delighted over his obvious worth to his family and formative country, he was happiest exercising effective use of horse and wagon in this manly overland teamster job. He developed internalized methods of responding to the world, and he tirelessly championed a Zen-like focus that demonstrated his affinity for following instructions without taking groundless risks. He intentionally advanced with a clear analysis and knowledge of the preferable routes and conducted his business bravely and confidently, even while traveling at night.

There may have been something special about Clermont County, Ohio, that influenced the distinguishing character of the region. This county was central to the surreptitious affairs of the Underground Railroad, for one thing, and to the groundswell of Northern support for equality and liberty for all people. It was impossible for men like Ulysses's father not to be politically involved with the pertinent issues of the nation locally. Jesse shared his outspoken idealism with his neighbors and especially with his son. It can be no small coincidence that the county the Grants moved to and lived in for years was also the home turf of passionate Union supporters William Tecumseh Sherman, Philip Sheridan, and George Custer, among others. Ulysses Grant, like Abraham Lincoln, found able assistance from an extraordinarily large and loyal home team, not in Washington or New England but in the rugged and discordant western territories.

Even the eastern, propriety-minded citizens of Windsor were no moral equivalents then for the less patrician, freedom-loving pioneers who ended up going farther west. Noah, the social desperado from Connecticut, for example, married Rachael Kelly from a righteous Pennsylvania Quaker community and continued farther west. Their constant travel companion was Noah's half brother from Coventry and Ulysses's steadfast uncle Peter. Peter was so devoted to the freedom of slaves that he became the president of the Kentucky Abolition Society after the Missouri Compromise. As others left Kentucky to the enabling slave traders and slaveholders, Peter refused to move on, staying put while many people of conscience crossed over the Missouri River, migrating to territories like Ohio that were still totally free. The Grant family was in an imperative position to assist a network of supporters of the Underground Railroad by moving people seeking asylum to northern, free territories and states during Ulysses's formative years. The Grants did so as often as good judgment would allow them to safely do it.

Young Ulysses readily became adept at earning the trust of people of all political and social perspectives. All through adolescence, he had exhibited an uncanny natural ability even to calm wild horses. It was natural for such a daring young man to develop the trust of others and be trusted. He responded instinctively to the best in others while refusing to react to impropriety, as he often needed to do, with horses or some dominant people.

Ulysses always had a favorable opinion of horses, and he communicated his respect for people just as naturally. He favored any chores related to the quality care of horses, and he likewise appreciated everybody's contributions to a worthy end. This trait complex enabled his excellent service as a quartermaster in the army and in other leadership roles. He could not place a finger on exactly when and where he developed the unusual sensitivity needed, but this natural grace always seemed somehow mysteriously present from within his very spirit.

As the reliable eldest son, Ulysses usually gave unconditional responsiveness and respect to his parents' wishes and was aware that he modeled mature behaviors for younger siblings. He did all that could be done to meet expectations, and he earnestly sought positive recognition and approval, which were rarely granted freely. Hannah and Jesse expressed appreciation for Ulysses's contributions to the family by withholding corporal punishment. He savored the feeling associated with continual unspoken trust, but he sometimes wondered why his parents were so resistant to recognizing his goodness with overt expressions of parental pride. He disdained the discomfiting thought that he could be speciously taken for a fool, or simply for granted, by the very benefactors of his altruistic, often amiable, and generous efforts on their behalf.

Animal death and butchery were foul but necessary components of Jesse Grant's frontier business. Along with generally undesirable grim toil came accompanying wealth and a measure of frontier political capital for the intractable father. Jesse was authoritarian and often as narrow-minded and selfish as they come, but he also became influential in the developing community of Galena, Illinois, more than 300 miles up the Mississippi River, as a wealthy business owner, and enthusiastic, articulate, and patriotic editor of a regional newspaper and even the first Republican mayor of Galena. Among other things, he had a poetic bent that entertained potential business clients by naturally self-promoting himself and his craft. All of the father's affected communication not only kept people coming to purchase luxury items from his retail outlet in Galena, but also may have also helped Ulysses get his hand on a dependable job for the first time after leaving the army. This was more poetic justice for Jesse since he had used words and political acumen to secure the critical congressional appointment to West Point, and the world-class college education that the future president had always desired. Jesse hadn't had the opportunities for formal education that his son enjoyed. Through self-education, by reading all the books he could get his hands on, Jesse modeled for Ulysses a strong, decisive desire to learn, through compulsive reading, and determined self-improvement.

The young Ulysses had habitually made it clear how invested he was in his own personal enrichment through reading every book available to him, or by attending itinerant teachers' classes at makeshift schools as they came to town. His bent for self-improvement and his yearning to please his parents were readily apparent, but any overt recognition of these qualities came to him without fanfare, as a distinct surprise. For example, his father simply announced one day that Ulysses was going to the US Military Academy to get a college education. Jesse would certainly benefit financially from educating his son at the taxpayers' expense, but his motivation appeared to be mostly for the benefit of the professional enrichment that a West Point education would offer his praiseworthy eldest son.

Ulysses wrote in his autobiography that he initially thought he would not go, for he was certain he would not be a good soldier, but that he also knew he certainly would go if his father said so. Jesse approved of what he saw in Ulysses. The father, an avid reader and writer, had no formal education but impressed upon Ulysses the importance of getting one. He articulated in poetry and prose what was most important to him and what he thought should be made more permanent. After he moved his family to Georgetown, an attractive place offering strong inducements for business enterprise, Jesse wrote:

> **I continued on in this way, improving a little every year. Two years after I built my house, I added a kitchen in the rear, and a few years later, when the increase of my family required and my means justified it, I built a large house in front. My object was not to get rich, but to make my family comfortable and contented, and to train up my children for usefulness. Early in the year of 1839, when my oldest son was nearly 17 years of age, he told me he could never follow me in the tanning business; that he did not like it. I told him that whatever he expected to follow through life he should engage in now, and not waste his early life in learning a business he did not intend to follow. Among other preparations for life he desired an education. Although my business had been good and reasonably successful, yet I did not feel able to support him at college. So I suggested West Point; that met his approbation, and I made application, and by the veriest accident in the world I obtained the appointment for him.**

Prior to this, Ulysses had had no personal intention of making a professional career in the army. Even after graduation from West Point, a unique and prestigious institution of education established for America's most gifted men of the day, he presumed he wasn't one of these exceptional soldiers and would be at his best not as a soldier but maybe as a professor of subjects he liked, such as mathematics, geography, or art.

Jesse had learned the tannery trade from his father Noah's enterprising half brother Peter. Drowned at an early age in the Missouri River, Peter by default left his nephew Jesse all his business interests and obligations related to tanning. To make matters more difficult for Jesse, his father was a serial disappointment as a farmer and was consequently unable to profit adequately from any enterprises on the frontier, so he ultimately could not support or elevate his own children. This meant that Jesse modeled himself after his more successful uncle. You could correctly say about Jesse, without exaggeration that he "pulled himself up by his own boot straps." He did this without any help from his father, or at least that is what the hardened and disdainful Jesse often thought.

Jesse didn't really do too well until he moved farther to the boundary of the western wilderness to start the tanning business anew at Point Pleasant, Ohio. He married Hannah Simpson, an aloof and stoic Kentucky girl, on June 29, 1821, ten months before the birth of their first son, the future US president.

During their lifetimes, most ordinary family people recalled homily and hearsay and a long tradition of attention-grabbing stories about their relatives and their own experiences, person to person, one cohort to the other. Specifically, the Irish, Welsh, and Scots were well-known cultural storytellers, having earned that distinction by supporting shared values, keen political awareness, and passionate idiosyncratic alliances during thousands of years before the written word. These family stories were stuffed with habitual and practical concerns of kinship, empathy, kindness, poetry, and cultural insight for their subjects, the very considerations that are often sadly lacking in many family relationships today.

This habit of storytelling was certainly true of the Grant family, and there is much more information about his heritage that even Ulysses could have known and justifiably considered for his memoirs. And the verbal family characteristic set the stage for the most telling distinctions about Ulysses as he made his way toward high-ranking manhood.

Throughout his life, even as a boy on the frontier, Ulysses squarely faced threats from farm boy bullying. He maintained fixed engagement against certain truly contemptible antagonists until they surrendered. His distain of social unfairness and bullying appeared to come naturally, or so it seemed to himself. The propensity to take charge in unpleasant social scenarios was an mystical endowment like that of a survival instinct. This dynamic characteristic dramatically foreshadowed unusual effectiveness in dealing with ordinance and leadership of men in the rapidly advancing years of war and peace. It's certain that he was a highly trusted, passionate, and sensitive man who often suffered quietly, but he suffered with a larger intellectual perspective than that of many contemporaries, and he only did so in an extraordinarily self-disciplined, calm, and effective manner. Likewise, he summarily faced the risks of a frequently burdened professional career with a laden efficiency and dogged persistence tailored from survival and progress on the western frontier and experience as Quartermaster in the Mexican War.

Ulysses Grant evolved into a keen, sympathetic observer and a diffident storyteller who could effectively pull off telling a good innocuous joke to those family members and career associates closest to him. He listened, too, intently so, and was resistant to normal fears because he had assimilated legends of bravery about his Connecticut grandfathers and cousins who had fought in all of America's battles alongside their plucky and practical but stalwart Connecticut Yankee peers. He was a believer in his parents' pioneering patriotic acumen, true grit, and self-respect. He held dearly to the origins of his honorable New England soul, and he had the theater to cleverly use humor to exhibit his brilliant no-nonsense and commonsense understanding of important issues.

Grant was a man well suited temperamentally for the highest leadership roles in the army. Looking back, it was as if he had been born for the role he assumed in the Civil War. He became intentionally inclined to nurture his talents as a protégé of two generous career warriors who came before him, General Winfield Scott and General Zachary Taylor. He admired Scott's ability to inspire men generally and to listen and communicate with them one on one with thoughtful consideration and genuine respect. He conscientiously emulated Taylor's ability to get results without displays of hyperbole or a great fuss. Grant would become highly regarded for his ability to listen to all sides of an issue, consider the weight of the different arguments, and only then make his decision as commander.

The leaders he chose as personal mentors boosted his capacity to defer to passionate and patriotic differences of opinion on paramount issues. Sensitivity to such differences appeared to come from a birthright of family influences, including that of his mother, who, according to Ulysses himself, never judged or spoke ill of anyone. Remarkably, considering all the other stresses he managed, Ulysses Grant intently avoided making himself an unnecessary threat to others, whether friend or foe. He was often readily self-effacing and laughed heartily with others when he heard well-mannered, enjoyable, truthful, and culturally constructive yarns about himself manufactured and presented in his company. This quality helped make him into an uncomplaining, competent, and emotionally disciplined man with unparalleled strategic vision in war and peace. He could be trusted for his competency and goodwill, military or not.

Initially, though, and in the absence of a worthy cause to support, Ulysses S. Grant found that his personal emotional struggles, such as his obsessive rumination over delayed news and mail at isolated outposts far from home, coupled with his lengthy absence from family, provided ample room for career uncertainty and instability. Soldiers were typically assigned to remote outposts for two or three years at a time, particularly early in their careers. Most, if not all, became jaded and took to whiskey drinking, tobacco smoking, and card playing to pass the long, indolent stretches of time.

Whiskey, the drink of choice for frontier soldiers, was particularly intoxicating to Ulysses Grant. At that time, serious logistical problems associated with ensuring that water was potable made many intelligent people habitually distrust water as a healthy resource for their hydration. Since contaminated water had been linked to many a feared malady, including premature death, water was not considered to be the healthy alternative it is today. For most of human history, wine, beer, and other alcoholic drinks, such as whiskey, have been considered safer alternatives to the dubious supply of untested water. Ulysses heroically tested and proved hypotheses on this subject during his military service. Placed in charge of a trip through Panama to the West Coast before any canal existed, he directed his armed forces to avoid drinking the water as they worked to make a path through the tropical forest. He directed his troops to use wine and beer as substitutes for the local water supplies they found available along the way.

Julia had argued that she should be allowed to go along with him to the West Coast on the trip. He refused to take her because of the risk and potential for unforeseen consequences in the undertaking. Civilian laborers who, along with their families, had accompanied the army on this trip were not so well instructed. Because they had drunk unrestrictedly from local sources of water, nearly all were sick and dying of dysentery by the time they reached the Pacific Ocean. Only the soldiers under Grant's command made the welcome contact with their waiting transport ship unharmed and healthy.

A noticeably shorter man than most soldiers, Ulysses Grant simply embarrassed himself more readily by a conspicuous inability to hide symptoms of intoxication as well as many of his frontier companions,. When, as the barracks quartermaster in charge of garrison payroll, he was unexpectedly officially disciplined by a superior officer for consumption of alcohol, he considered his career to be unfolding incorrectly. The formal criticism acutely hurt Grant's standing in the army, or so Ulysses Grant thought at the time. He was already decidedly upset about the long distance and time away from Julia. In this sensitive situation, the senior officer's curiously harsh discipline destroyed the quartermaster's already damaged belief that he could have a meaningful future with the army. So just a couple of years before the Northern and Southern states divided in the dread Civil War, Ulysses S. Grant resigned his commission and left the army—for good, he thought.

Later, particularly during and after the Civil War, when his service was recognized and thoroughly admired, he was generously gifted hundreds of boxes of finely made American cigars. The United States, in particular the northern states such as Connecticut, manufactured and exported tobacco products all over the world. Unfortunately, in the long run, overconsumption of tobacco hastened the Union army general's death. After scores of well-wishing citizens learned of his occasional enjoyment of a good cigar, they sent boxes of these goods to him throughout his military and political career. Ironically, these gifts from supporters helped to bring about Grant's throat cancer, painfully extinguishing his life after his sixty-three years of otherwise auspicious military and political survival.

Cadet U. S. Grant, West Point, New York, 1840

CHAPTER 12

Cognitive Dissonance

Preschool Sensibility and Awareness,
Reflection on Fatherhood, Quality Education,
Authenticity and Authority, and Finding One's Adult Voice

GIVE ME CREDIT FOR BEING inquisitive, and possibly a little more than just an irrelevant afterthought as a child, even though my father responded to me sarcastically more than once. One of his put-offs was, "A fool can ask more questions than a wise man can answer." Or in response to the honest question, "Daddy, why's the sky blue?" he responded, "To make little boys ask questions."

Unfortunately, that happened again and again. Once was actually too much. I could never again feel that everything was all right between us. Could he have known how acerbically I would take this sarcasm? It was so very difficult for me to assume precisely whether he could or could not. I will never know now because I never asked—I feared that if I asked outright, he would just brush me off by saying, "Well, that's for me to know and for you to find out."

Father typically assumed, very correctly, that I didn't know how to respond to sarcasm. I was certainly at a disadvantage then. I remembered his axiomatic responses. I supposed at the time that they didn't really matter, but I mulled them over for what seemed like forever until I could understand if not appreciate them. But in the long run, our interactions were not constructive, and it was under circumstances like this that I committed his facile demeanor to heart. As I became a man, I certainly did more listening than questioning, but I have always thought the proper use of words is naturally more generous, a gift for greater and deeper understanding and rewarding study, specifically for children. Of course, father may not have actually intended to be so unkind. Should he be given more credit? After all, he worked and paid most of the bills for many years. Perhaps he didn't have questions answered in his youth either.

He did feel gifted intellectually—he said several times that when he was a boy he was permitted to skip the second grade in the grammar school. By comparison, I was, at best, "just a late bloomer."

I might have done a little better in my elementary school if he had answered, "I honestly don't know why the sky is blue. Let's go to the public library and look that up." But no, it was not to be. I became a relentless daydreamer and an underachiever during the first decade of my life. It was much later that I knowingly used words for the superlative power they gave me to create awareness in others and to share the wonders of life with people who were responsive and authentic, the way a gifted father should be.

This personal experience taught me that a sarcastic response always leads to mistrust because it is cynical and mocking of the trusting party. No one enjoys being put down with a sardonic response, and anyone will eventually assume that the person employing sarcasm is not a friend but a foe who can't even be relied on to give a truly uplifting answer. A person who believes he's superior, or needs to think so, is mordant and scornful in a clever way. Taking someone seriously and responding in an earnest way is vitally important to a fulfilling relationship.

Being a keen observer is a very important trait to possess also. It was almost always important, I firmly believe, for me. But being incredibly well informed and finding an articulate voice in important matters was often frustratingly beyond my reach. I have always felt a certain lack of conversational scope, or personal knack, as if there were a trick I still didn't know but others did.

I maintained a posh torpor by never rushing to a quick response or by simply not visibly reacting to certain words or messages at all. I believed I adequately compensated by avoiding even a justifiable response to an intentional offense, and I never even dreamed of making less than a dignified or profound response, particularly one that was to be modeled or to be spoken aloud. More onerous though, in the long run, was my persistent inability later in life to be an effective silent self-moderator. Some friends observed a missing filter that would have arbitrated in favor of truly accepting others' genuine shortcomings and made me a more patient and beneficially responsive man. Inherently neither shy nor introverted, I consistently acted impervious and unaffected, but unfortunately I was abundantly scornful of the glaring limitations of others, even when I too had these limitations but felt that they were at odds with my sacred notions. I found other people's errors of omission as impossible to tolerate quietly, with a semblance of grace, as intentional slights. I justified and maintained self-righteous scorn for both.

Observing my grandchildren now, I find it difficult to argue that behavior is simply learned and not mostly inherited. At the earliest ages, children intuitively understand the necessary aspects of life, it appears. Children behave as if they have known a lot since day one and express themselves clearly to demand what they need, even before they can use language. Born with a repertoire of physical and mental abilities, they learn the particular adaptations and compromises we have assimilated as adults, but the basic processes of being human are simply inherent, or natural. What observer can forget the first time a child returns affection, exhibits fear, or demonstrates rage? Circumstances will always vary greatly, but a child's normal repertoire is responsive and predictable.

My passion to develop and share the principles and practices of appropriate family values with parents and their children has perhaps not existed forever, but at least a strong desire for improved knowledge about the "how," the "what," and the "why" of family events for properly rearing, teaching, and coaching children has been present in me as long as I can remember. Discoveries made about an individual's legacies in the context of family are important for future perspectives, reflection, contextual illumination, long-term alliances among brothers, sisters, and other family members, and even the success of joint endeavors ranging from family picnics to the profits from better business and economic trade.

This book began on April 30, 2013, my sixty-seventh birthday. Its beginning was a gift that has remained with me until the end. The first edition's foundation arose out of many diverse cultures and traditions and owes much to a long list of teachers who believed, as I certainly now do, in truthful education and improved understanding. I have felt subtly influenced by a familiar spirit. So the book took form gradually and organically in response to a series of cognitively stimulating biographies; in some other way, it is an autobiography that includes the chronicle of when and where certain clues about ancestors were discovered, uncovered, or serendipitously presented essentially anew to me by this unseen spirit. Through applying an idiosyncratic method and format to the leisurely exploration of a common ancestry, I have found that many lives became vital to the central themes that have taken their form here. I am aware of no other specifically intended biography made about one man almost entirely from a composition of briefings about authentic ancestral relations. This was simply due, of course, to a keen sense of kinship nurtured over a lifetime.

With this chapter, I've personally just rounded another corner in an unlikely but amazing physical, meta-philosophical, and spontaneously generating investigation of our lives. Why a particular focus on family history appeals to me so automatically yet apparently not to many others is still a mystery to me, one that is not yet fully explicable even now. Personally, I feel the incredible inspiration and the blessing of it all.

A contemporary, apparently compatible British cousin named Douglas Grant wrote to me that in the United Kingdom the Grants historically owned and operated ships and were traders with the rest of Europe over many centuries. They were a culturally diverse family, he said, made up of Jews, Catholics, and Protestants, but their worldwide trading company united them all. He said that even many loyal lifelong workers and business associates took the name as their own. The livelihood and social connections to each other must have been a private renewable resource for security, satisfaction, and the realization of significant external opportunities and challenges that kept bringing kin closer together, generation upon generation. The Grant name gave each individual a strong sense of meaningful purpose and cultural identity.

Well, you might imagine the immediate and total dissonance when other contemporaries take a more critical stance and challenge the veracity of confirmed knowledge about the Grant family. Asking pertinent questions and exhibiting a keen interest in insights would normally suffice. But on more than one occasion, I was asked, "What do you get out of it, writing a book about your family, anyway? My reply was, " A profound sense of gratitude for all those souls who have preceded us. I gain appreciation for all who have given us a life to live, and I admire their talents, the skills they've developed, and any resources they maintained that benefit us here and now."

Only those who are blind to others' gifts, or perhaps those who take them foolishly for granted, would perhaps need to ask, I remember thinking. Interest in the past and future is a persistent intellectual benefit at the very least, and I do certainly enjoy relevant historical discoveries that help us respond authoritatively and swiftly to the accidental slight, the calculated snub, the unnecessary rebuke. There is no satisfaction to be gained by tolerating malicious attitudes or censure due to somebody else's superficial ignorance, disinterest, envy, or shame.

Which, fortunately, brings me back to our central character. If I were to pick out one true character flaw or blind spot in the eye of our premier subject Ulysses Grant, it would be his difficulty perceiving a disloyal and dishonest person. His imperturbability and reticence when face to face with prejudicial attacks on his personal character would have led most victims to raise a red flag to stop the unwelcome annoyance without second thoughts. He raised a white flag implying culpability, and surrender, to the antagonists. But Ulysses was well known for ignoring and forgetting entirely those individuals who unduly offended him. He resisted any impulse to respond authoritatively, to defend and explain the offense. He totally failed to reassure friends of devoted family of the unspoiled character and lack of fault. He often erroneously and selfishly took for granted the adoration that his close friends provided. This great man simply chose to ignore untrustworthy, deplorable, and dishonorable people and their criticisms. In response to an unjustifiable affront, he would turn the other cheek and simply never speak of the disgraceful adversary by name again, if ever he had done so. This consistent behavior, although perhaps well intended, never gave comfort to his promoters or ever helped to resolve grievous smears against, by association, the family name. Enemies throughout this champion's vigorous and victorious career in war, politics, and peace often concocted fake news and intentional lies at no noticeable sacrifice to their own questionable reputations. If Ulysses had simply expressed his righteous indignation occasionally, with the same control he exhibited in other interactions, he could have called out and destroyed adversaries as thoroughly in peace and politics as he had done in war. Unfortunately, U. S. Grant's reticence on the issues that seemingly impacted only him left his most devoted family and friends throughout the nation in shock and in pain, and the angst certainly lasts to the current generation.

An example of this point surfaced in conversation between a former World War II five-star general and our thirty-fourth president, Dwight David Eisenhower, and Vice President Nixon. The vice president repeated malicious hyperbole that Ulysses Grant was a drunk. Eisenhower said, "I don't know how that could be true, Dick. Grant fought and won our country's most difficult war."

Moving away from the New England region, or even passing on to an ultimate, alternative, definitive, or permanent milieu, is for me unacceptable until the Grant family name and its grand history are fully understood and positively restored in the minds of those still living here. Our successors living now and in the future should not be prepared to accept any less-than-rightful honor for their namesake. In spite of all the miserable cynics and cranks of every age, and those on the wrong side of history who have treated U. S. Grant unfairly, I hope to apply my full awareness to making the world a more truthful, descent, generous, reliable, and comprehensible place than I have so far found it to be.

Ulysses S. Grant, circa 1861

At the 304th anniversary of the birth of Mathew Grant, in 1905, the son of Ulysses and Julia, General Frederick Dent Grant, addressed the Grant Family Association at Windsor in part by saying this:

> **I am very much delighted to come here and meet my kinsmen and the descendants of our common ancestors, the Grants, where they first settled in Connecticut and where I have heard the rumor that soon after coming here, and possibly on this very spot, a little colony collected under a tree, not having written laws, or a house in which to meet and discuss the promulgation of ordinances, resolved that they would live according to the laws of God until they had time to write better ones.**

I have thought a great deal in the past and present of this family of ours, the Grants, and the descendants of Matthew Grant, and I understand there are about 9,000 now living and running through the book that is written on the subject. I fail to find a single case where one of these descendants were disreputable. It seems that all of them were what we call decent and respectable people.

Now it seems to me that where a family of that sort exists it would be well if they were united and exerted their influence throughout the country in the way of good citizenship.

From the godly sect that separated from England for religious and political freedom to my own parents' generation, it was virtually inconceivable to reason aloud that there was not a better life awaiting in heaven, particularly after people had sacrificed, rationed, and shared everything on earth. Life was much too brief, and the mission or work was all too great, not to be rewarded beyond the severely limited dimension between one's birth and death. It's difficult for us to imagine how our ancestors thought about death because our experiences are so different from theirs. The end of life was often anticipated as a blessing of bountiful rewards for the performance of a strict, narrow, but honest civic confidence. Faith and trust were attuned with daily munificence, sufferance, and sacrifice. That's what faith is—the belief in something you can't see but still sense or hope is true.

These ancestors could feel the consistent satisfaction of personal responsibility by living with faith in a just and transcending power, an alpha and omega that resembled the best-known rewards of living, love, care, and sanctuary, through poetic prayers and collective devotions. The idea of an honest, individual, and direct relationship with God often even negated the desire to find higher levels of satisfaction among the living on earth, or for that matter to find any motivation or inspiration in the secular knowledge and natural lessons that life had to offer.

Dad exhibited a strong commitment to family when I first knew him. This commitment seemed to have incrementally evaporated by the time that I was eleven or twelve years of age. Robert was six or seven. Our youngest brother, Steven Paul, wasn't even born until February 14 of that year. But I remember riding on my father's shoulders at the age of two, happily impressed by the worldview he gave me at such an unaccustomed height. I fondly remember our trips to go swimming at the lake on very hot and humid weekday summer nights after he had worked all day at a promising job in engineering with Hamilton Standard, a division of United Technologies. He took me to a football game at UConn and to see the Red Sox's baseball games at Fenway in Boston. He knew how to instruct a kid about sledding and ice-skating, too, in the winter months. There was a time when I believed he knew everything and when everything he did was very breathtaking and wonderful.

These were extraordinary occasions that were important and venerated by his presence. As he worked himself closer to the transformation from a vital aerospace employee of industry to a holy man of the Methodist Church, everything seemed to change for us, and not for the better.

Dad was particularly worn out from a week of work when he was still working five days a week at his old career and became an assistant pastor on weekends at the First Methodist Church in Hartford. Working seven days a week was restrictive and felt like sufferance for us all. After church and dinner on Sunday, at about 1:30 p.m., he usually fell fast asleep on the living room sofa, evidently very satisfied and at peace in his incomparable world. I reflected on the missed opportunity to get to know him better even when we were still all together.

In retrospect, I realize that our father didn't talk about any of his concerns about living moment to moment or day to day. In fact, he didn't appear to have a plan for sharing with us or getting the most from life here with us, even when we overtly offered adulation. I'm almost certain that he inherently and passionately believed that there is no sanctified relationship in the whole universe other then that of an individual with his creator. He insisted throughout his life that he "had been called to the work of the church." Once, when I was a teenager, Dad pointed to a painting on the church Sunday school wall and reflected on the title, *Christ Above All*, as embodying his own philosophy in a nutshell. He was called to go somewhere special, and he took us all along on this mystifying, uncertain, twentieth-century spiritual trip. Family temporal existence and worldly issues were always an indecisive, tacit afterthought to the besotted vicar we called Father, and we were all naturally hurt by his remoteness, daily detachment and apparent indifference much of the time. There was a "calling," and then there was an accommodating, devoted family. Our father did something that he had told his sons *not* to do. He often cautioned, "Never put all your eggs in one basket."

Mother held the family together like glue for years, while we were all living under the same roof, by making sure we were at the dinner table together during the evenings and on Sunday afternoons after attending church. These activities were very important to both parents as we prepared for college and gradually, one by one, left home and their care for good. Unfortunately, important everyday issues, such as our common passions and our aspirations for the future were rarely discussed. After we were mature enough to appreciate adequately the authenticity, openness, and honesty that our family dynamic demanded from each of us, the family unit had hopelessly changed, precluding the possibility of any real formative communication. Sadly, we never made the appropriate transition from becoming independently self-actualizing and respectful of all family diversity without the palatable presence of specks of scornfulness obstructing mutual love, a deeper awareness of how we were related, the many points of possible lasting agreement, and why these things mattered. Dad never thought to express and act on the conviction that a family that actively plays together works much better and much longer together.

Unfortunately, when Mother died at fifty-seven years of age, in 1979, from the ravages of breast and uterine cancer, Dad was certainly no more in the present with us, days and years after her burial. That time for more closeness was quickly lost. Unfortunately, he somehow never managed successfully, or made it a priority to include his children, or even loving grandchildren, in important aspects of an on-going family life. Somehow, though, he found what he did need, and remarried within a year.

Due to his example, it is hard for me to not imagine as the most extreme irony of all existence the almost universally belittled and taken-for-granted though also most lovingly inspired construct, that of the family. All of his education and career aspirations somehow appeared at perpetual odds with durable and abundant family satisfactions. This was so much so that to me it was overtly mind-boggling and frustrating not to experience familial love and trust as the center of our lifelong affective growth. But even then I could never quite understand the often-quoted maxim of despair expressed to me by others, "One can chose one's friends, but not one's family."

Unfortunately, I have always tacitly criticized Father concerning what felt like his abdication of a father's vital responsibility to remain in touch with his children. I never talked with him about my disappointments, but do certainly wish I had tried more persistently. As it turned out, for many years I was distrustful and scornful of selfish, reserved, aloof, and superior-acting men who have their heads, let's say, up "in the clouds." My disdain for unauthentic, patrician, and emotionally inexpressive relationships became so much more intense after Mother died. She was the mirror image of a father's love then. We have always missed her.

Even if we arrive at such differences in interpersonal outlook and approach by intent, or through unintended sins of omission to each other, it is common knowledge that we all still share DNA from a great many generations and are often literally closest in behavior to our parents in extremely important ways. We share a physical commonality over generations through the family.

It is also true, though, that we actually could be more similar to an unknown grandparent from two or more generations ago and certainly never know this without persistent interest in family relationships.

Decisively, we must be audacious and provocative with the people closest to us, in the moment, in order to introduce them gradually to larger differences and worldly obtained values, to maintain compatibility with them in the long run. Freely sharing thoughts and concerns between loved ones leads to greater, lasting understanding and trust rather than the opposite effects of increased misunderstanding and growing distrust. No matter how intense views may be at any moment, the focus on being in sync with others is a critical human filter for all states of reality from basic aspects of security to self-actualization and commitment to lasting proprieties that are greater than oneself. Mutual communication is the cornerstone of decency.

DNA will not make likely total harmony between the relevant and expectant in living from day to day. It isn't easy to be a successful, model parent or a master of your own family-related destiny. But in the end, indifference and scorn are terrible spiritual ends for anyone, with or without a family.

A focused imagination, organically grown insight, refined perspectives, well-made plans, and passionately honest communication translate to a more alive and honest nuclear family. I have learned that true compassion and long-term, meaningful family connectivity require from all participants the most mature communication skills. There is so much more room to love those in life who help you magnificently express yourself and to realize your self-worth in their generous company.

As a family, can we discover meaning and purpose in any particular aspirations and characteristics found among our common ancestors? Are the inspirations that we discover to have animated our ancestors still holding close the affinity we need for living our own lives? How are we similar to others in our past? How are they arguably any different? Do we have the ability to perceive and choose the diverse realities useful from one age or epoch and apply them to our own? Or is each of us the solemnest and most independently sanctified entity to evolve from the conditioning of his or her own isolated time?

Being no more than five feet six inches in height, and weighing 150 pounds at that time, the wily young adult captain Ulysses S. Grant proudly flexed the sturdy build of a carpenter during construction of his first house as a husband, a house that he passionately called his home. In good humor, he anointed the new place, his first chosen pursuit outside service in the army, "Hardscrabble."

Ulysses's work as a family man was cutting down mature trees and firewood to hearth-size lengths, splitting the wood, neatly stacking it, and allowing it to season, for family purposes of survival. Then he sold any surplus for five dollars a cord to his fellow countrymen in the frontier city of Saint Louis, Missouri. The average homestead used four or five cords of wood for heating and cooking a year, so the purchase of this abundant store of energy was a difficult business from which to work steadily long hours and extract much profit. A cord of firewood has always been four feet wide, four feet high, and eight feet long, and Grant's only tools in those days were a couple revered hand-sharpened metal axes and saws he had been able to find rummaging through his father's forsaken tools and at frontier estate sales. Fortunately, Ulysses's youthful, renewable strength, indomitable determination, and imperturbable self-sacrifice, along with the early help of his friend and father-in law's African servant, provided tolerable conditions for accommodating this unreasonably tough and all-too-common vocation for a propitious man.

Ulysses couldn't realize that his grandfather and great-grandfathers (the Noah Grants) had lived similar lives with few or no different results. If he had reflected on the complex that was uncannily repeating itself over four generations, including his own, he may have comprehended a little sooner the unprofitable path he was so woefully on then.

Captain Ulysses Grant had truly distinguished himself through his assertive action and bravery in the war with Mexico. He had left the army that had prepared and educated him professionally, wed Julia Dent, who was in all ways an unusually engaging, delightful girl with him, and unwittingly returned to a state of obscurity. Ulysses drew together his only assets from land that his father-in-law, Mr. Dent ("the Colonel"), had endowed to him through his marriage and parlayed them into a less than satisfactory and sufficient sustenance. It was a regrettable situation known too well by the insightful, hard-thinking Jesse.

In those days, the Grants always had too little or no discretionary income. Ulysses admired beautiful and expensive horses, and the Colonel had always provided the finest house and blessed his daughter Julia with beautiful dresses that she now sorely missed. But Julia and Ulysses's difficulties were their own difficulties, and the burdens and work they shared together made their common bonds all the more powerful.

Because of his own financial worries, Grant had little time to offer Jesse and Hannah for any perhaps long overdue consideration as a recipient of their lifelong support. It was all he could do to avoid the temptation of asking his father for financial aid. That is, of course, with the exception of one occasion when there was a national recession; Ulysses was out of work, broke, and facing the likelihood of starvation. Ulysses had no place to turn but to his seemingly always fiscally creative and solvent father, he thought. Suffering to overcome his anxiety and loss of pride, he wrote a thoughtful letter, asking timidly, politely, and perhaps even a little too circuitously for money. He offered repayment of the loan principal at a much too generous interest rate. This alone may have somehow upset or even angered Jesse Grant, who normally wrote back when written to but on this occasion inexplicably ignored his son. This was the beginning of supposed hard feelings from the point of view of the struggling, disadvantaged and worried son.

Ulysses Grant was an implicit strategist in the army. He was an aggressive, athletic, and persistently proactive planner. At home, with family, he often went to bed late and woke up at sunrise, motivating himself silently: "What is the most important thing I can do today in order to make life better for those whom I love, and for those who love me?" No one but Julia saw this side of the man.

Through much of his civilian life, he was joyful when he could put enough food on the table for his wife and infant son. Grant was content and fortunate to do so because he could at last be with them and be happy at home. He reasoned that, through no fault of his own, he could not be in more than one place at a time, and he now chose home. He gladly played "piggyback" and other childish games with his first infant son. He was a good father to the boy, and he was willing to take on any and all work offered him for the family good.

In a few years, after continuing to eke out a physically and somewhat emotionally punishing existence at the Hardscrabble farm, Ulysses Grant moved on with his young family for a more promising occupation, writing, "Since leaving St. Louis I have become pretty well initiated into my family's leather business and like it well."

A sister-in-law described Ulysses at the time as having the physical strength to "throw the frozen hides down the chute for them to be cleaned and distributed. The Captain could take a hide that weighed over two hundred pounds and throw it with a fling of the arm, whereas Orville [her husband] could not, nor could [another brother] Simpson." She continued, "He seemed like he was meditating on some project all the time, quiet, a composed man. He didn't laugh so much aloud, but smiled with his eyes."

As a child suffering from a natural and, I thought, near-terminal fear of speaking out loud in the classroom, I didn't know what it would take to become an effective public speaker. I figured that whatever this quality could be, I did not have it whatsoever. Controlling my breathing was never a thought that came to mind. The question was, rather, would I breathe?

I could not visualize standing up before peers and adults and being reasonably articulate with a natural flow of words. My body responded with distress and panic, unconsciously and uncontrollably releasing tiny rivers of sweat that would run down my neck and soak my shirt front and back. I learned that my neck quickly turned crimson, too! No one bothered to tell me how to effectively control my breathing, look over the heads of the audience, avoid self-defeating thoughts, or even thoroughly plan and prepare my speech in advance of the actual event. I never observed a teacher do this in class or a parent do it at home.

In modern, technologically advanced times, communication was perceived as becoming increasingly important in American culture. A developing sense of inadequacy was inevitable for those with no natural predisposition for public speaking amid the ever-increasing, overwhelmingly rapid development of new communication technologies and inventions in poetry, novels, movies, television, telephone, and the preferred modern forms of music, jazz and rock and roll. I was so ready to learn how to learn.

Finally, because of my perceived scholarly deficiencies as well as my particular emotive potency, I emphatically chose a profession and mission after excelling in a single subject in my senior year of college. The subject was educational psychology, a discipline that concentrated on making learning all things much easier. Out of 221 students in the lecture auditorium, I received the second-highest grade for a near perfect performance on the midterm and final exams combined, and later I earned special recognition for my surprising superior potential as a graduate student of learning theory. Something mentally mechanistic and motivational clicked into its proper place in that course and made me aware of the implicit value of teaching all the skills of "knowing how to know." I also became an avid reader of the self-help books of the 1970s and '80s. I was thrilled to learn that I could be as smart, or perform as well academically, as others when I applied insights from learning theory and other closely connected study skills on a habitual basis.

How mysterious and ironic that I had spent all the previous years of my life searching for meaning, yet I discovered the keys to success only at the very end of my exceptional educational journey. The only acceptable explanation was that after all the years of self-punishment, discouragement, lack of direction, and unreasonable frustration, the answer would be all the more smartly practiced and appreciated for what it was: a dedicated new destiny to become self-actualized and to rise above my previous complex of self-configured limits. This became my particular reason for being: to instruct myself and then others in the most effective and efficient learning processes, and then to teach myself and others how best to employ psychology in the implementation of practical teaching and learning methods. My teachers could not teach learning theory in the elementary grades because science hadn't yet discovered enough about the human brain and the natural processes for effectively using applied knowledge when we were in school. This knowledge would change the trajectory of my life and the lives of others in a positive way. Mastering appropriate scientific approaches to understanding the human brain through secular psychology and education advances could be employed in the future to end "elementary school daze" like mine.

Previous Grant family members may have used language too judiciously, both scrupulously and cryptically, but I wanted to be a bit more expressive of sentiment than they had been. I admired great social leaders like the Indian leader Mahatma Ghandi, the African American reverend Martin Luther King, Jr., and the brave American Harvard graduate John F. Kennedy. All who combined passionate purposes and a sense of justice while being true to themselves and humanity were my heroes and heroines. My champions were figures who exemplified our human potential to fundamentally change the world for the better. Ghandi said, "Be the change you want to see in the world," and that was by far the most amazing and the noblest thought I had ever heard.

It often helped to remember that Ulysses Grant suffered from all the physiological and behavioral symptoms we call stage fright. This personal agony had control of him for most of his life, but particularly during his elementary school days. The wholesome Puritan notions of modesty and humility appeared to dictate that he could not call attention unnecessarily to himself without some important reason to do so, or falsify a story even slightly for personal gain. He listened attentively and respectfully to other children and believed every word to be sincerely and literally the unvarnished truth. His early challenges in the classroom seemed to be centered on a single distasteful task, that's been called in my time, **"S**how and tell."

The young boy found interesting what others in his class had to say. It was too easy to think of others as the intellectually brighter ones because of their natural glibness in class.

His difficulties also stemmed from his sensitivity and mindfulness. Nothing really interesting happened to a boy in Ohio in the early 1800s, or so he hopelessly thought to himself. Every other boy or girl he knew went to school and lived an uninteresting life—very much like he did, he thought.

So when Ulysses Grant was unaided and put on the spot, an uncharacteristic panic disabled his ability to think of even one thing so different or special about himself that would interest anybody. He was unable to even imagine embellishing upon the banal, incapable of telling a lie to exalt himself, to relieve his suffering just a little bit. This quandary could never motivate him much, but he would pay a price for his reticence. He was bullied, measured as simple or even dull by some of his most asinine playmates at school. Some even called him "Useless," coining this nickname as a nasty, flimsy wordplay on his proudly given name, Ulysses.

Advancing years would prove Ulysses a very much more sensitive, intelligent, mature, and appropriately morally inclined person then he may have first appeared. He became in all ways the opposite of deficient or insufficient and developed his characteristic fervor, but he never came to like public speaking.

At West Point, he naturally fared better, given the honest delight that he obviously found in subjects like mathematics and geography. Such subjects came more naturally to him than to many of his classmates who had come from all over the United States. He began to sense that he had something special to live for within the realm of higher education. He also developed further the affinity horsemanship at this prestigious academy.

Much later, though, it still quietly mortified him that standing in front of his peers was so inexplicably uncomfortable. It was still even a bit embarrassing, though his strengths were now finally being both perceived and acknowledged.

In the midst of his rare public speaking episodes he bizarrely felt his pulse quickening beyond direct control, his neck turning red under his tight blue collar, and more than a bead or two of sweat slipping off the ends of wet hair follicles and rambling indecisively around and down the back of his neck. Fortunately, in one instance, he correctly massaged a page of notes in his hand and concentrated on speaking the few coherent sentences he had prepared on official Washington hotel room stationery the night before. These notes would save him from betraying his lack of confidence at the nineteenth-century White House and would enable, as a simple matter of duty, an honorable speech.

At this very moment, expectant American congressmen were intent on tapping into Grant's unknown but reputed potential to save the Union. He was to lead loyal citizens' armies against all their rebellious brothers. Heretofore, no other man had been given more responsibility, or higher rank, in the nation's professional military command.

As this undersized, sinewy, brisk, but seriously devoted young soldier stepped up for a cameo soapbox moment, at that great national instant, the president's secretary recorded this honest, ample, and straightforward statement from Grant:

I accept the commission with gratitude for the high honor conferred. With the aid of the noble armies that have fought on so many fields for our common country, it will be my

earnest endeavor not to disappoint your expectations. I feel the full weight of the responsibilities now devolving on me and know that if they are met it will be due to those armies, and above all to the favor of that Providence which leads both nations and men.

Lincoln was pleased by the message. He was pleased by the brevity and natural reticence of Grant. Later, the president said, "He's the quietest little fellow you ever saw. He makes the least fuss of any man you ever saw. I believe two or three times he has been in this room a minute or so before I knew he was here. It's about so all around. The only evidence that you have that he's in any place is that he makes things git! Wherever he is, things move!"

CHAPTER 13

Critical Judgment

Reflection, Maternal Lines, the Judgment of Critics,
Respecting, Rectification, and Resolution

PERSONAL OBSERVATIONS AND ACTIVE PARTICIPATION in receiving and interacting with the history found in this research are earnestly desired and appreciated. The reader's own discoveries, recognition, and awareness of intellectual and cultural resources will supplement and corroborate what's been already researched and reexamined. Active interest in a continuing, incomplete story is necessary in historical research due to the great swaths of time and events that pass and the immensity of typical topics of concern between reciprocally receiving minds. You can only imagine with sincere enthusiasm all the material you will bring to a topic for yourself and others as you discover it and acknowledge the useful past in the years to come. Similarities we share have a greater impact than minor differences, which are seldom perceived more than temporarily. Perhaps that is the case partly because every couple that has children sheds alienating differences as these differences become less important with continual acceptance of diversity and trust.

Information found in this record is limited to past ancestors who have been prominent in the diverse grassroots of America. Maternal families made American history and folklore too, of course, but this particular story has been somehow quite extraordinarily empowered and fortuitously inspired by the direct paternal path it so happens to have taken, either by chance or by design. It often seems to have been independently driven by what I interpret only as coincidences or road signs from forces still hidden to all of us. It has made me consider the processes I suspect to be metaphysically associated with an ethereal propinquity dwelling simultaneously with me in tranquility and peace, though a little on edge, especially in the atmospherics of the Connecticut River Valley.

Perceiving from within waiflike comfort zones the weighty complexity of genealogical research into family ancestors is not an insubstantial experience or one for simple cowards or imperceptive fools. Most people are intimately knowledgeable about, or can remember without too much mystery, the lives of their parents and grandparents. Just about everyone under twenty-five years of age typically has a couple of living parents, but an in-depth knowledge of the family in toto often appears eccentric and esoteric.

Simply put, many of us may remember four grandparents and some interesting aspects of their lives, but it certainly becomes much more intense to think about having had eight great-grandparents, and of course sixteen great-great grandparents. Even though all of us have had, as the only typical possibility, thirty-two great-great-great-grandparents, and so on, we are not accustomed to considering this even upon the occasion of a family reunion. A family legacy like yours and mine holds at least the potential to be significant to thousands of cousins. For example, Ancestry.com indicates that I have at least five thousand cousins in the United States—ours is said to be one of the largest families in the world.

When two long heritages intersect and combine, it is truly an extraordinary wedding. The exploration of family ties is a task much larger than that, one that can sometimes be satisfactorily explored only across the length of a book or even volumes.

It has been difficult to identify the salient facts of the lives of my dearly meaningful maternal grandparents, Thomas Young and Louise James Young. I have found that the Youngs immigrated from the northern border of England, the coal-mining country of Durham County. When we visited Scotland in 2015, I observed that the countryside on the border of Scotland and England looked almost identical to the land chosen for settlement in Pennsylvania by my maternal great-grandparents, John and Sarah Young. It is filled with rivers and streams and with mountains of coal. My parents, Howard and Helen, visited South Shields, Durham, when I was preoccupied with graduate studies at UConn—my keen interest in ancestors of the Young and James families never reached its zenith in those days, as it had already done with the Grants. In fact, it was just this year that I've been fortunate to penetrate the crust, connect the dots, and realize a little bit more about the origins of my maternal-line families.

It was a difficult eight-hour ride by car from Hartford to the former Young family farm, where our immediate family of five resided. The farm was located by a picturesque country tributary near Wilkes-Barre, Pennsylvania, nicknamed "the Falls." Mother, who grew up on the family farm with her brother, used this nickname. Perhaps it was her grandfather, John Young, who first discovered the lovely natural water falling from lofty, sharply stratified plateau ledges with even more impressive water falling to swimming pools below. The waterfalls were unforgettable, but the family farm wasn't freely talked about at all—I think grandfather Young was happy to give up farming, sell the property, and move to Hartford to work a non-farm job on the assembly lines of the Pratt & Whitney Aircraft Company during the Second World War. Grandmother worked there on the assembly line also, and they moved to a new house built in Glastonbury, Connecticut, in 1955, ten years after the war. They had a nine-hundred-square-foot rectangular ranch-style house built for $14,000; they made the down payment by collecting on Uncle Tommy's life insurance policy after World War II. As you have already read, Tom James Young was unfortunately killed in Normandy on June 8, 1945.

Mother worked as the secretary in one of Hartford's historic retail enterprises, a rug company that sold domestic and imported rugs. When Helen L. Young married Howard L. Grant, one might have seen the mutual HLG initials as a sign made in heaven and even predestined in some way. I sure was happy to be born into the family and came to appreciate living in America, too. My life was full of potential. Of course, I know now that we are hardwired to generate metaphorical thoughts that appear to support, justify, and enhance existence. Still, I would be lying if I suggested that this metaphysical sign wasn't significant to me or to my parents. Mother was the one who seemed most convinced and significantly proud of this circumstantial or supernatural token of approval.

Throughout my career, one of my goals has been to be constructive, to write and teach about rewarding, positive human potential. It is in my character to find suitable metaphors and hope that fellow descendants can enjoy them and grow intellectually and emotionally from hearing accurate stories. We must treasure and assimilate any knowledge about family in order to gain an appreciation of similarity and diversity everywhere.

It is usually a pleasure, and only occasionally a greatly unanticipated embarrassment, to uncover facts of authentic family history. Everyone must find a way to address the momentous slight or spirit-damming malfeasance, no matter how intensely egregious.

Where mistakes were made, let us avoid repeating those erroneous and notorious flaws again. Where abilities and talents have been authentically present, perhaps hardwired in DNA, let's use our advanced knowledge of these similarities to increase auspicious goals and successful encounters in well-planned futures.

On Friday evening, December 13, 2013, while meeting a hometown resident socially for the first and last time, that person said, "Thomas, I understand that you are related to Ulysses S. Grant."

Initially delighted by that true but extraordinary recognition, I answered affirmatively and inquired, "Why do you ask? Are you related to him also?"

The individual shot back in return, "No, but I am related to an ancestor who lost his life fighting for the South in the Civil War. They lost everything, you know! My family was even wealthy until then."

Fortunately, being prepared and predetermined to confidently address this hurt and apparently piously damaged woman, I agreed about how terrible the Civil War was and how much people suffered and lost on both sides. I gently added that the Grants were wealthy at one time too but lost their fortune in the Revolutionary War.

At another time, more recently, I was quietly looking at an artist's sketches, cartoonish abstractions of Ulysses S. Grant in pen and ink, displayed by the Museum of Modern American Art in New Britain, Connecticut, when the head curator hustled by, interrupting, "Oh, that's Grant! He was a drunkard, y'all know!" He just as suddenly disappeared into a gallery without saying another word, perhaps ignoring the scornful expression I made at him. I was just about to howl out loud when my wife, Susan, quickly warned this insolent and supercilious man, "Oh, careful, Thom's related to him!" But the scamp was already gone.

A painful psychological Grant-family public relations nightmare emerged—I recognized it gradually during my lifetime, as perhaps other Grants have done over and again many times since the passing of Ulysses. As life ground forward for our nation after reunification and his death, the family kin have shouldered the burden that doggedly persists pertaining to Grant's universally under-appreciated life. The dimmer lights at prejudicial levels of our tribal humanity often foil all discretion, replacing pure understanding with worthless bigotry. In this case, sensitive Grant family members can relate to being the potent targets of disproportionate reproach.

The Grant Family Association held annual reunions for many years in Windsor, Connecticut, from the late 1880s to 1929. There is no record of Ulysses S. Grant visiting this historic old hometown of his sixth-great-granddad Mathew Grant. Ulysses understandably had bigger fish to fry as president of the United States. But there's reason to believe that Ulysses knew about these early Grant Family Association meetings in Windsor and his historical Connecticut ties because his sister was photographed attending at least one such event during their mutually shared lives.

These family reunions were a wonderful opportunity for local and distant cousins alike, since so many had migrated across the United States, participating in the search for freedom, new adventure, and sources of happiness and prosperity over the years. The participants at these reunions first went to church to worship together and remained after that service for large and small discussions about family history and current events. Before quitting for the day, most would dine together and attend to the keynote address about the more or less audacious old saying, "How great it is to be a Grant!" Those in attendance over the years listened to crafty and humorously delivered speeches or historic commentaries on their European and American ancestries. Most of the distinguished speakers authentically and intentionally romanced the family, taking advantage of a receptive audience that had caught up favorably on smiling family providence. They dined together and visited family burial grounds, toured centuries-old homes in Windsor, East Windsor, South Windsor, and Wapping, and sometimes even revisited family now located in other contiguous communities of the Connecticut River Valley like Manchester and Tolland.

Remarkable as it may seem now, the Association missed the opportunity to employ the novelist Samuel Clemens, a personal friend of President Grant, as master of ceremonies at their Windsor event. Clemens, or Mark Twain, a highly admired Hartford writer, humorist, and publisher, might have roasted the president in Windsor as he had once done successfully at a New York City business luncheon. His comments had both his audience and President Grant roaring with uncontrollable laughter at the performance.

The Windsor Historical Society Museum bookstore has recently sold its stock of many old surplus issues of the Grant Family Association's reunion programs and family magazine. The museum librarian said a year ago on my visit there that she appreciated how much the town owed to Mathew Grant for awareness of early Windsor history. She knew that he was the original parish recorder and the town's second first selectman for more than thirty years. She graciously said to me, "Mathew Grant is responsible for nearly all we know about Windsor during its formative years."

Fortunately, I knew that too, thanks to an incident that had happened no fewer than thirty years previously, during a weekend research expedition. The assistant pastor of the First Congregational Church of Windsor, which is located directly opposite the Historical Museum on Palisado Avenue, had loaned me a handwritten copy of Mathew Grant's town clerk diary. I earnestly tried reading the entire journal off and on for a little over a year, with little success due to its antiquity, and then returned it to the church. The pastor directed me to simply put it back where he had found it in the center foyer coat closet of the parsonage. I did just as instructed, but I felt very uncomfortable returning such a family treasure to the shelf for hats and other accompaniments. It would have been wrong to keep such a historical treasure, though I was temped to do so. My latent Puritan ancestry argued that it was against the church rules, and particularly one of the Ten Commandments: "Thou shall not steal." In the final analysis, I was convinced upon reflection that it would be more regrettable and painful to steal it than to let it go, albeit sadly. I knew that my old conscience would always suffer with guilt if I didn't give it up. Even Mathew Grant's priceless journal would not be worth that amount of suffering for the remainder of my life.

In spite of apparent appreciation by almost everyone, no one, to my knowledge, has fully examined and authoritatively acknowledged the direct family relationship of a founding father, Mathew Grant, to the great commander in chief of the Union. Even during Grant's tenure as president of the United States, no one, apparently, acknowledged this high-ranking historical relationship; nor has anyone else at any time in four hundred years. I mean to say that not one monument or other worthy link has yet been made honoring President Grant in the historic old town.

In contemporary East Windsor and South Windsor communities, this has been handled in approximately the same way—by not being officially addressed. A local resident is credited with maintaining the record of members in our great-grandfather's household in Wapping. This loyal old-time resident and neighbor of founding families kept a card catalogue at home for related purposes. The catalogue is now housed at the Memorial Library and Historical Museum on South Main Street, South Windsor. I hope that local heroes like this gentleman, Barney Daly, will be remembered for their kindness and interest in the rich local history they grew up into as children.

When visiting the Windsor Historical Society and Museum on my most recent trip, I met a lifelong resident of Windsor, an actual past director of the Society itself, who indicated that she was related to the Grant and Loomis families. She verbally poked me and quietly prattled, "Well, Ulysses S. Grant wasn't considered a very nice man or a good president, you know."

I realized that this attitude was based on hostile rhetoric that was prevalent at the turn of the twentieth century, when it sadly became fashionable to support the Ku Klux Klan to the detriment of the national honor and of recognition of freedom and cultural diversity for all. Ulysses Grant's leadership recognized that "justice delayed is justice denied." So after the Civil War, President Grant continued to fight discrimination. Many former slaves gratefully acknowledged him, as they did Lincoln, by taking his worthy surname following their liberation. Knowing much about the life of Ulysses Grant, I was once again delighted to be able to respond as firmly as I did at that instant: "You should read the newer biographies being written about him." I sensed her disadvantage and added another fact to consider: "Grant was the most well-regarded and loved American of the nineteenth century."

This misled woman was clearly sidetracked by irresponsible biographers of Ulysses Grant over many years, from the early 1900s up to the 1980s. For four recent generations, revenge-filled character assassins came out of the woodwork in force and spoiled the truthful memory of Ulysses Grant. These included southern authors and other bitter opponents of his presidential policies of social reconstruction and of freedom for the black and white alike. It was fashionable to examine the victor's record with extreme prejudice and bias, which went hand in glove with a particularly reactionary, racist, and revisionist political era, the early twentieth century.

Grant was elected to two terms in the decade following the Civil War because he was trusted with the important changes to American culture for which the war had been fought and won. In a way, it was the perfect irony: U. S. Grant had spent the better part of his whole life fighting against the dandy patrician, the fraudster, and the economy that fostered racism. He staunchly defended voting rights, political equality, and justice for all Americans, and he is still judged by people who should know better, at least by now in the twenty-first century, as "not a nice man."

A successful effort was made to belittle and bring into question the principled personage of Ulysses S. Grant. Men and women who should have known better began to rewrite history to assuage their real or imaginary personal suffering, their profound sense of guilt for disrupting the Union or for fighting so vehemently for what patriots like Grant challenged as the greatest "unnecessary, unwinnable, and unworthy cause." Unfortunately, even some blood relatives, as in this last instance, have failed to defend Grant and his name against the character assassins of the previous century in our country.

Throughout his life, Ulysses Grant behaved in ways that ultimately led him to become an influential person and leader. Peculiar greatness was within him—it was developmental, and he demonstrated this fact in the fortuitous twists and turns of his life. From an early age, he instinctively opposed the oppressors of his day who would wrongly presume power and authority over others. As a youth, he was not a bully—he was the opposite, an authentic, truthful, strong, and principled young man who was able to consistently and firmly but fairly put true bullies in their place. Grant's leadership was shaped as much by character as by intelligence. As a young man, he had became a competent military strategist as a graduate of the US Military Academy at West Point, and he characteristically maintained a specific distrust for the all too common politicians of his time who masqueraded in spotless, well-pressed uniforms, seeking undue recognition as dependable military leaders. As a daily practical concern, he was competing with many men who were ill suited and unprepared by either training or experience to lead soldiers into the great war of his time. In sharp contrast to the assumptions of many would-be authorities, he was well prepared by generations of family patriots before him for the realities of a military career.

When asked what I might call my book, I said that the title could be *Saving Grant* because throughout my whole mid-twentieth-century life, I had come across Americans who would discount even Grant's most worthy contributions and question his fine character, even rudely to my face. When I mentioned this to my daughter on one occasion, she said, "I've had that happen to me too! I think it's a shame."

It is insulting to many generations of trusting Americans that they have been hoodwinked by malicious untruthfulness and perfidy directed at them generation after generation. It is time we all realize that it was inappropriately trusted writers and self-proclaimed authorities who made the unjustifiable effort to advance and sustain the unsupportable premise that Ulysses S. Grant's unremarkable civilian work indicated that he was little more than a common man made great by extraordinary circumstances. Though intentionally discredited by some, Ulysses S. Grant is a solid example of an uncommonly gifted, well-prepared American who shaped the great military victories of the Civil War, to the lasting benefit of the nation as a whole.

Grant was the inheritor of the DNA of civil champions, individuals who had distinguished themselves through the risks they took for our country from even before its beginning. Through trial and error, and superior intention, Grant's are typically great Americans. Even some good biographers have not exhibited an intuitive and genuine understanding of the national gift of Grant's great promise, and the blessing of his devoted fulfillment of it as a trustworthy civilian, family man, soldier, and statesman president.

In stark contrast to Ulysses Grant's ballyhooed alleged lack of potential during and after his own time, Robert E. Lee was the well-known inheritor (through marriage) of George Washington's Arlington, Virginia, estate. Ironically, many historians have readily appreciated Lee for his greatness as an endowed leader for the South while casting a jaundiced eye at Grant.

Grant's long, deep, and meaningful association with American military history is all but unknown to most Americans. Distant disrupters of truth and their incomplete or inept scholarship have largely failed to examine adequately the historical connections of Grant's inherent or inherited leadership capability. Even more characteristically, angry, sectionalist Southern white men have succeeded in bringing regard for Grant down to the level of their own empathically impoverished stature by their failure to relate intuitively to the victor. What has been sorely needed is a public validation of Grant's genuine brand of leadership; his ability to see the whole American field of battle militarily and civically; his broad intellectual vision; his steadfast sense of purpose; his passionate, progressive drive and determination; his definitive superior awareness of geography as manifested in his apt use of maps and math, strategic planning, and silent and secret maneuverings; and the long overdue full acknowledgement of balanced consanguinity and civic affinity. Grant was as strong and as authoritative as he needed to be, given his unconquerable pedigree, but no less or more so.

A Post–Civil War Grant Family Portrait,
Washington, DC, Circa 1868

CHAPTER 14

Abundance

Ecological Origins, Prehistoric Stone Age Culture,
Trade on Inland Lakes and Rivers, a Garden Metaphor, and
Renewable Resources

CONNECTICUT IS KNOWN BY RETIRED friends, who travel worldwide often, mostly by airplane, as the "salad-bowl state," since it can be clearly observed from thousands of feet in the air that most of the land is covered by mature green tree life, unlike more barren and uninhabited regions. Connecticut was home to forests and many seminal species long before its geographical separation from Africa, millions of years before human evolution was even anything considerable enough to speak about.

Immigration has brought every kind of kindred peoples to the American continent. The first people were here fifteen hundred thousand or more years before us.

The Europeans who settled in North America from the year 1620 forward discovered mature communities comprising hundreds of enchanted, productive, happy natives who had explored and prospered through exclusive use of their land: the rivers, forests, hills, and valleys that they had initially found uninhabited. For thousands of years, groups of humans progressively and successively migrated among magnificent plants and animals. Tribes lived together in times of peace, and in these periods they enhanced the environment and the quality of life side by side in these natural surroundings.

Since the early seventeenth century, a great many foreign settlers have brought their habits to the land. They cut the wood and split, stacked, seasoned, and burned it for survival. They hunted animals for food and to rid the forests of terrifying or troublesome beasts, as was the practice in Europe. The results of aggressive colonization, fervent farming and hunting, industrial development, and worldwide trade of precious natural resources have consumed and virtually eliminated all the mature indigenous plant and animal species in New England for an enduring period of generations.

Though Mathew Grant was instrumental in family successes, his original community of Windsor has fully prospered in its own right over the past four hundred years and has produced many benefits to the state of Connecticut since that time. It is today an old, authentic, and distinctly diverse American community. Connecticut had its roots deep in the colonial period, and it is now much greater than a seminal parish community of a single ethnic group. Windsor has provided satisfaction to everyone seeking a free society with important organizational principles deliberately adapted by the state of Connecticut from the purest influences.

Lately, and only lately, we have observed a significant number of larger carnivores such as black bears, foxes, coyotes, mountain lions, hawks, and even fearsome-sounding fisher cats beginning to re-inhabit the forests in Connecticut. For a whole lifetime—mine, namely—forests have been silently and effectively regenerating to maturity and becoming a suitable habitat for a diversity of these large animals once again.

Incidentally, what are called telephone poles today, though possibly not in your future time, are increasingly being used for the sad purpose of posting homemade signs seeking information about lost pets, which have likely fallen prey to this incredible resurgence of diverse species. Happily, most of us today welcome the broad diversity and abundance of life that nature freely brings to us. This said, the fisher cat is a possible exception for the moment due to its fearsome shriek, which woke every normal human being in the neighborhood late last night.

We have stepped back in time for a moment. Earlier today, April 30, 2014, was the fourth annual planting of a vibrant family vegetable-and-herb garden along the bank of the Farmington River. All that is needed for the essential roots to grow in abundance are days of normal sunshine and the customary nighttime intermittent rains.

Not all weekly patterns of weather are beneficial for a garden. Two years from now, we will experience an unusual series of very dry consecutive weeks in May, June, July, and August 2016, and we will have to work successively harder and harder to water with our manual labor in order to save everything already planted from the drought. After this particular year, we decided to plant our garden only if rain was predicted in the weekly forecast.

But in the present, Susan, my best friend, private confidant, lovely spouse, and girlfriend since our sophomore year of high school, has quickly transplanted a couple dozen small verdant seedlings, which were purchased from a wholesaler in Southwick, Massachusetts, the day before, to the propitious family garden by about 11:40 this morning. This annual garden planting was accomplished efficiently between the two of us in about an hour after breakfast—I allow twenty-five minutes for the pleasant drive to and from home to the garden and thirty minutes for the actual work.

In this annual spring-to-fall activity, we each only actually work for a half hour at any one time, but the delightful garden, of course, benefits from a whole hour of our labor. That's the way I have come to think about our marriage, also. When we work together, the essential activity makes up less of the perfunctory, profitless routine, and we each share the rewarding, pleasant things in life more. In the garden, some of the credit for this unanticipated relief can be attributed to the town of Farmington, which has tilled the soil well, enabling our planting by disrupting, at least for a week or two, the growing patterns of the clever weed seed that is already dormant and hidden in the soil. When working as a couple, we are in all ways a proficient team, if not perfectly compatible gardeners. The only problem seems simply to be that, as the eldest sibling in my family by five years, I was always left in charge. In her childhood, Susan was also the eldest and the bossy one.

In reality, neither of us would be motivated to do much at all if for some reason the other was absent from our life together. Year by year, our mutual trust and overriding joy have grown, paralleling an increase in our satisfyingly coordinated actions. This can also be said for our mutual assistance to grandchildren when our daughters and sons-in-law are all at work on weekdays. We normally pair up for childcare and oversee any combination of delightful grandsons, Matthew, Cameron, Ian, Rhys, and granddaughter Calla. It's hard to imagine any painstaking or joyful endeavor, including traveling anywhere, without sharing all the love. Love is granted more, the more that its given away.

One of my fondest and most frequent memories is the recall of how much love we have shared over the years. Perhaps that is why I relate so much to all the stories about the lifelong romance of my extraordinary cousin Ulysses Grant. He and his lady, Julia Dent, shared passionate, abundant, and durable affection for each other. As a young lieutenant, he would regularly—about twice a week—ride an army-issued horse to her house from the frontier fort where he was stationed after graduation from West Point. He did this as long as he possibly could before his two-year involvement in the Mexican-American War made it impossible.

On one such trip to Julia's place, he found a normally dry riverbed swollen with water from heavy rains in the mountains. He even wondered if the horse and he could get across the deep, fast-moving stream safely. If he had had suitable options, he recalled, he would have taken one of them, but after carefully considering all possible action, he decided not to turn around and go back but to attempt to ford the hazardous stream. Arriving soaked to the bone in his best uniform, dripping wet from head to toe, he became the cause of much laughter and admiration from Julia and her mother. Julia and Mrs. Dent always saw something extraordinary in this young man who expressed steadiness and devotion.

Weeding a garden is another all-consuming routine, the unpleasant circumstances of which are equally hard to avoid. Once you plant, you can't just go away and neglect everything important. Different fellow gardeners, though, have a variety of methods to reduce the danger of unnecessary work. The procedure Susan and I favor now to avoid an excess of unwanted weeding involves the purchase of a small garden cultivator. I use this to carefully till the soil between rows of plants as the garden matures. There is something chaotic and determined about weeds that would certainly take control if the garden were left to nature. Any weed will grow faster and taller than any carefully nurtured plant.

Of course, we use a hoe between plants after cultivating the rows. Naturally, we weed by hand closer to plants to avoid inadvertent injury to them. Weeding is not an intrinsically enjoyable aspect of gardening no matter how you do it, and it is not avoidable if you want a healthy, productive, and beautiful garden. Hearty and steady growth, robust plant maturity, and the justifiable gratification of nutritious food made more plentiful are all more likely with pertinacity.

It is approximately two weeks later than what is normally considered customary for planting from seed, the very beginning of the planting season in this particular region. Prior to this week, there was inclement weather that led to flooding in the meadow plateau along the river. Planting is postponed almost every spring by even the most devoted gardener until the flooding ends.

Following a period of hard rains, spring days normally become evenly separated by days of sunshine, crisp dry air, and cool evenings that are ideal for farming in Connecticut. Enjoying the net gain of physical flexibility and the spiritual fruits of one's labor makes gardening indispensable in retirement. When one is in such an atmosphere, it is impossible to deny the old adage that I intentionally memorized while observing the skills of a familiar planter, my grandfather Thomas Young: "Man is closer to God in his garden than anywhere else on earth."

By comparison, the local Methodist church in East Hartford, where we eventually exchanged our wedding vows at just twenty-two years of age, was the Sunday morning sanctuary for our parents of the 1950s. We were still wholly uncomplicated infants. It was there, in church, that I am aware of first encountering other kids. One baby girl in particular was nice, very likable, and attractive to me, but I didn't know why that feeling was so keen. That baby girl was, of course, Susan Jane Stephenson.

Susan and I were born in the same year, 1946, so we've certainly been peers and virtually in the same postwar baby boomer playgroup our whole lives. (Depending on the decade we're talking about, though, that playgroup could be more appropriately called a "party group" later on.)

She was born on September 3, and I was born 127 days prior to that blessed event, as you already know, on April 30. In temperament, we are mirror images of each other. If I see an issue a certain way, usually ardently, she very typically takes the opposite, less keen, but often more erudite or sagacious stance.

This has a lively impact on our normal communications. In other words, I've often gotten progressively agitated, she increasingly defensive. Our close adult friends, Bill and Anne, have remarked that this generally seems to work for Susan and me, and I agree that we have certainly always been indubitably united, in the long run, by something more corporeal than mental.

Susan's mom, Mittie Chapman Stephenson, was my preschool supervisor during the church service on Sundays. I cannot recall all specifics about the other children, or even about Susan for that matter, but Mittie must have commented to Mother that I spent the whole hour in Sunday school sitting with folded legs, seeming to find interesting the image of a yellow duck embossed in linoleum on the floor. I know about this because, in a nutshell, it is all I heard about the Sunday school later.

Fortunately, from my point of view, I remember intentionally willing my intrinsically alert but mute, small infant self to demonstrate incredible strength of character for a little baby, arousing excessive physical and mental balance for the unbearable amount of time it took mother to return from the service upstairs, pick me up, and release me from imprisonment in the spot where she had planted me on each of these Sunday visits. Since mother assured me that she would be "right above me" in the church service and "right back," I kept looking up at the ceiling, particularly when startled by the big church organ booming with all the excessively joyful parents singing a little too loudly.

The initial impression actually made on my future relations was not exactly the first impression that later in my life, after reaching puberty, I would have wanted to make. I was certainly too uncomfortable, quiet and unexpressive, but apparently, because these qualities weren't so out of place in church, they failed to prevent the flowering of my most essential future adult relationship in life with Susan. I'm always grateful for that.

As youngsters, Susan and I lived in neighborhoods on opposite sides of the town of East Hartford. She grew up in the north end of town and I in the south end, but I felt close because of church every Sunday, even when we had no actual contact. When a cousin visited a couple times from Pennsylvania, Susan was the only girl I ever thought enough about to visit. So my cousin Buddy and I rode bikes over there to see her, kill time, and be vaguely in touch. Susan was always kind enough to help me amuse my teenage cousin even though the conversation was always a little awkward for a while. That was about it. We went to different elementary schools until attending the only high school in town, and we dated steadily from the end of our sophomore year on.

At the tail end of our sophomore year, I obtained a license to drive a car and was granted the use of one to commute across town to high school. I also took a part-time job on weekends.

The family car that I used exclusively, with parental permission, was a one-year-old, previously owned, metallic blue, meticulously detailed 1961 Ford Futura. It was the newest thing for a family to own two cars back then, let alone one car. But with this car, I would significantly augment the family income to support my relationship with Susan and my aspirations for a future that would include college education.

I obtained house-painting work, the work that I needed to justify continuous use of my wheels, by word of mouth from people who knew my parents and by extension, me. Our family dental hygienist, for example, recommended neighbors of hers in Wethersfield immediately after I finished with her small ranch-style house. Susan's brother John helped paint houses in Wethersfield and in Newington that summer, working at the rate of two dollars an hour.

Dr. Ryder, DD, my family dentist, hired us to paint his house in West Hartford the following summer. So we eventually painted houses in West Hartford for several summers, as well as in many of the towns in Hartford County on both sides of the Connecticut River.

This was a time during which father applied his artistic talent as a tool designer at Hamilton Standard, a division of United Technologies Corporation (UTC), in Windsor Locks, and later as a production supervisor in the towns of Newington and Manchester for smaller independent tool-design and manufacturing companies. All the while, he attended the University of Hartford as an evening student for eight years to earn a Bachelor of Arts degree. He soon after made a critical transition from tool design and engineering to the work of an ordained minister of the United Methodist Church. While in the pastorate at the North Canton Community Methodist Church, he also graduated with four years of studies from the Hartford Seminary Foundation, securing a Bachelor of Divinity degree; later, he earned a Master of Sacred Theology (MST) degree from Yale University while ministering full time at his next church, the North Haven United Methodist Church on Clintonville Avenue.

Despite his distinction as a serious scholar of the Bible, and in particular the New Testament, he did not advance quickly toward the top of the Methodist Church hierarchy because of his late entry into the profession. As a direct consequence, he never was paid enough to adequately support an earnestly tithing family with three sons. But the church provided a place to live that we all called home, albeit hardly in the permanent sense of the word. It wasn't clear after the complete transition just how enough income for a satisfactory future could be earned in the family, but the mastery of a trade and some serious physical work, like house painting, appropriately matched my ambitions in those days.

In my worldview, the whole scenario seemed very unique and challenging and vaguely unpromising. It required a lot of planning, willpower, and especially physical exertion, which was considered at that time to only make boys stronger. As the eldest son, I naturally intended to set a strong example for my siblings, to be conscientiously considerate, almost selfless and simultaneously self-actualizing. Preferring to work alone at my craft, I didn't normally like asking for help. I exuded confidence in obsessive myself, and I became more motivated over income than normal. I grew trim, more powerful physically, sharper mentally, and generally more robust than most of my friends and family thought of being.

To earn what was perceived as nearly two or three times the going wage for a youngster's time and labor, I felt motivated to take on jobs almost nobody else seemed to want to do. I remember often thinking altruistically about what my father had said to me: "When the going gets tough, the tough get going." So with this often in mind, I ultimately proved through highly productive work activity that it was possible to earn money for expenses and pay for a college education and an engagement ring, though I sacrificed the experience of a carefree, or at least an emotionally satisfying, late childhood development. Tough and determined, I eventually succeeded; however, in the process, I also sacrificed important family events that are traditionally highly prized by loving friends, siblings, cousins, parents, and beloved grandparents.

The painting business started for me at home while Father was at work or studying for his profession. I began at only fifteen years of age by working solo on our small five-room colonial at 660 Forbes Street; shortly after that, a quiet, previously unknown neighbor, who lived almost directly across the street, watched me painting and asked Mother if I would be interested in the job of painting his house. Earning the attractive sum of $350 on that job was enough to excite my entrepreneurial calculations for hypothetical future fortunes in business during all summers from 1962 well into the '70s, even while I attended college and graduate school full time at UConn.

House painting naturally also enabled me to develop physical strength, superior balance, and gross and fine motor dexterity throughout the long process of moving the heavy wooden ladders around, and climbing with the intensity of other primates. I also developed fundamental business abilities, the skills of a trade, and confidence, though with no mentor in the field, I had developed little capability to effectively lead other people as an employer, manager, or boss.

The little blue Ford Futura went one hundred thousand miles all around the capital region of that modern state, on both sides of the Great River. It often had a ladder or two on its top. All the while, my considerable physical accomplishments and a keen passion for living kept nurturing a rising exultation and the anticipation of climbing toward life's apposite rewards.

CHAPTER 15

Purpose and Identity

How Others View Us, Predisposition, Big Ideas,
Distinction and Decency

YOU COULD BE WONDERING IF you are related to certain immigrants or how those to whom you are related are important to you. Of course, this is not something you think about every day, but in a rare carefree moment it may be natural for your mind to leap at the chance to explore old ground and check present inventory, maybe not even any ever-present physical resources but the historical, and gain a greater sense of perspective about your life and your latent hidden potential.

I remember the first time I expressed an interest in our family's historical roots. It normally seemed entirely too presumptuous to start a conversation in this way, but one day I asked a kind artist, Uncle Corwin Grant, if he thought we were possibly all somehow related to Ulysses Grant. He told brothers Robert, Steven, and me slyly but self-assuredly, "We're all related somehow." This seemed somewhat too simple at that moment, and we all shared a nervous snicker, but this all too reticent answer persisted to instigate further a madly growing curiosity that would be further resolved only by investigation.

The Grant surname, as something I had in common with my contemporary relatives, was only a tantalizing small piece of a genuine puzzle, or the beginning of a mysterious, slowly revealing, protracted intellectual brainteaser in the exploration of family history, ethnicity, culture, and the quiet, persistent processing of a certain labyrinth of readily obtainable factual material. In other words, I did not go searching for much information in the beginning. Later, determined to discover the meaning of our family name, I made a lifelong practice of willfully collecting and assimilating as many clues as possible from familiar surroundings and spirited local links with predecessors and the past. Aided by intuition and an indomitable purpose, I little by little revealed and intently explored a probable pattern of historical family ties, and with further research I was usually able to verify those ties, too.

In the very beginning of my exploration, many ancient family names oddly appeared to mean something in particular. I learned that many surnames, such as Woodman, Miller, Mason, and Smith, were originally given to signify an address or occupation. A parent could tell a son or daughter simply, "Run to the Millers' for a jar of flour." Of course, other names denoted other relationships—for instance, the son of Stephen might be surnamed Stephenson. Other names, like Goodwin, signified certain event outcomes. And some names, like Grant, could even be descriptions of physical or character traits. This name has been given by prior generations to describe either a well-reputed or eminent man, as in the Netherlands (Grandt), or a great or big man, as in France (Le Grande).

Today, one may sense a new definition rising on the old brand of Grant. It is a newer late twentieth- and early twenty-first-century perspective and a considerable paradigm shift. I admit that I—perhaps alone, at present—now consider the name Grant to mean "gift," and to signify especially a gift with some special significance or influential intent.

CHAPTER 16

Appropriate Aims

Perception of Purpose, Metacognition and Big Notions,
Trust and Diffidence

EVEN THOUGH IT WAS A long time in coming, a new consideration for
the family surname of Grant will not be at all surprising to the twenty-
first century citizen, who will probably consider it as having always been
the case. The new meaning is not likely to diminish greatly in significance or return to the old meaning exclusively for a long, long time to
come, if it ever will. Because of the changing and expanding role of
charities, corporations, and of government in the lives of the people, exceptional gifts or grants from the commonwealth for the common good
are increasingly sought and provided for a diverse and growing number
of reasons and causes.

My surname was a solid place to begin to explore the fact that most
of any family history, its complete, unknown, authentic and metaphorical mass and shape, is hidden from our common senses under all forms
and levels of more immediate, uniquely vital, or secularly current and
urgent learning experiences. The mastery of various trades and disciplines, for instance, will consume much of a young adult's time and
resources and unfortunately delay or prevent the meaningful analysis of

long-term family gifts and ability patterns until a time when these patterns are perhaps sadly less useful or pertinent late in life.

If this chronicle aids any individual, it is likely to create an early method of reference though which that person can contextualize his or her attributes and capabilities in terms of longer-term perspectives and aims. For instance, if you prefer visual learning rather then auditory, you may appreciate identifying the brothers, sisters, or cousins of different generations with the same bent. If you shy away from public speaking or some other skill, you could find knowledge and even comfort by embracing similar tendencies in your overall hereditary background. Our five year old grandson Ian can carry a tune remarkably well, but Ulysses never could and he was aware of it. One would be likely become a beautiful singer, though with the other, not so much could be expected.

Nature evolves slowly but relentlessly forward toward improvement—it never purposefully retreats, but it is up to each person to identify promising bundles of his or her human potential and to make individual improvements. Severely limited by the sequential natural order of individual events and by our five sharply limited senses, human understanding requires the application of reason and the artful analysis of a large amount of buried data to give us the most desirable long-term view for living in sync with the laws of nature and our own special secrets of propitiousness.

Most people privately believe in things they cannot readily perceive, and we can all be more open to the possibility that there are faculties and realities that we do not ordinarily experience. Simple faith that someday all will become known and experienced in superior detail has long been the historical cornerstone of conscientiously educated and spiritual lives. There are always more truths in life to appreciate and comprehend, but the sooner we discover our particular truths, the better.

Most people could live now, as many have in the past, without feeling remotely connected to family precedents. For example, one could ignore any impulse to live in ways that are consistent with the ways of former generations. Most of us have very little sense of presentiment about the future except through, at certain times, our own children. Most of us struggle from one day to the next to make incremental advances in an unrefined, indistinct, or absentminded circumstantial context. This is, namely, ordinary living, and it includes fulfilling a series of vaguely acceptable temporary roles with little immediate gratification. Normally, we will work to make life a little better each day for ourselves and for those who love us. We work within our conscious spheres of influence. Belatedly, if at all, a few aware people exalt a metaphysical sixth sense with reference to how they fit seamlessly and painlessly into the dark matter of the great cosmic puzzle.

Many people finally learn to make peace with the universe despite ordinary obstacles and setbacks; alternatively, some people just can't be happy and live without feeling the nagging sense of anxiety that something from day to day is not quite right, always missing, or hardly living up to reasonable expectations. We can usually get along with a strong belief in a relatively transitory cause, or something seriously perceived to be much greater than ourselves. We simply learn to be in sync with extrinsic powers that appear to enhance our human existence. Seemingly intrinsic personal characteristics such as "being honest to a fault," "fear of incoherence in public speaking," and "fear of radically improving one's health" are painfully derailing. Continually improving matters in the cosmic continuum depends on self-determination, persistence, a better knowledge of our place in time, and an awareness of the many other forms that we could have experienced. We can experience a sense of immortality if we think of our lives as extensions of the lives of ancestors, lives that resonate a certain unique and authentic truth.

Unfortunately, in the final analysis, it is sure that some ancestors would rather be forgotten than forgiven. We are often much more willing to forgive than to forget them. The last event these ancestors would welcome would be to have relatives still sifting through the big erroneous zones of their lives, specifically moral ones, a century or more into the undisturbed afterlife. Others would graciously appreciate and encourage familial interest in learning from heritable archetypal shortcomings.

Father told me, "All is fair in love and war." If this platitude is true, most of our ancestors could joyfully and equally deem even their most audacious and shameful stories illuminating. This particular aphorism of powerful victories was always so very perplexing to me. Obviously love and war are complete opposites and mutually exclusive in every way, though perhaps not so much in terms of the gravity and the weight of human behavior and its consequences, which become exponentially weightier over generations.

Until I wrote this book and reflected on everything I have already discussed in it, I didn't understand that dad was seriously affected to his soul by the ruthless robbery of his uncle's Irish sweetheart. It was never spoken of, so there are few details I can relate about it, but there were some things unspeakable about brotherly betrayal, and my grandmother Grant, that were taboo family topics. The incommunicable consequences were inherently passionate and powerful, satisfying both of life's strangest exigencies--- those of love and war--- or of building up, and tearing apart.

I now realize that father was actually very fearful that anyone, even one or all of his three sons, would usurp his personal life space or place, as he knew his own father Howard, Sr., had done to Corwin. This became more apparent and observable when dad married a woman twenty years younger than himself after mother's devastating struggle with cancer. Thinking uncle Corwin had lost something priceless, and that he had remained a bachelor his whole life because of it, our dad linked this somehow to the ancient Greek legend of Oedipus, particularly in his declining and defensive later years. He knew well this love-and-war story about his own flesh and blood. Living in the past, as he often did, he reacted in a way mysterious and misunderstood by us. A perverse and sad fear had replaced first-rate familial trust in his relations with sons, but even worse for everyone was his secretive impulse to cover up his fears and behavior in total silence, and erroneously isolate himself and his second wife from his family.

CHAPTER 17

Grandparents

Generosity, Wisdom, and Moral Authority

PRESIDENT GRANT BELONGED TO THE eighth generation of descendants from our immigrant forbearers. My generation is the twelfth. As individuals, we come and go, sooner or later. Our family has been around at least as long as mankind has recorded history. If all family, present and past, had never died and were still living in one great place, the diversity, similarities, and abundance of parents, grandparents, and cousins would be immensely more evident than we can imagine now. Each person would be significant to us, and the qualities each person would demonstrate would inspire lessons about our actual, bountiful, and rationally and culturally diverse existence, an existence much greater than just one life. Just think of the projects, careers, and experiences of life we actually could and would likely share.

We have discovered, like many grandparents, that it is the most subjectively refined joy to know closely all the children in family. Taken out of momentary context, we are all amazing, lovable, entertaining, right and wrong, appropriate, clearheaded, and overwhelmingly constructive. We are all forgivable. There is no known satisfaction that even comes close to that of enjoying glowing interaction with lovable children or to a loving infusion of grand family to life.

You, too, will be honored in the way you show respect for your forbearers. We must tell all children our memories about their great-grandparents! Otherwise, how quickly we separate and become sadly divided.

We are all lively and productive at the moment, able to enjoy the beneficial results of previous positive choices by our grandparents, parents, and ourselves. We have auspicious prosperity and happiness to an extent most of our ancestors could only envy, or dream of. We have reaped these family joys by standing on the many shoulders of our parents and grandparents, as our ancestors too did. From the blessings of careful planning based on the enlightenment and endurance of our familiar heroes has come the steady rise and grateful recognition of intergenerational generosity.

FOOD FOR THOUGHT: YOU ARE NOT JUST YOU!

NUMBER OF US IT TAKES TO MAKE YOU:

Family member	Number of us
You	**1**
Parents	2
Grandparents	4
Great-grandparents	8
2nd "	16
3rd "	32
4th "	64
5th "	128
6th "	256
7th "	512
8th "	1,024
9th "	2,048

10th	"	4,096
11th	"	8,192
12th	"	16,384
13th	"	32,768
14th	"	65,384
15th	"	131,072

Howard Leslie Grant, Sr., offered the sweet-spirited, bright-blue-eyed assurance of transgenerational understanding and bigheartedness in his pleasant sixty-something face. Even as he smiled with ancient family eyes and greeted the impressionable small child with sensible silence, a steely stillness if not quite calm serenity, he communicated honor and stately command of the mixed company during our few family visits. Grandma Rebecca Noble Grant sorted through all the smaller details in conversations with mother, but it was grandfather who appeared to be the most mildly accommodating, strong, and authoritative figure. Sagacious moral say-so was characteristic of the male adults in the generations I was exposed to as a young boy. Moral authority was still, at the time, underscored by acts of physical aggression, such as a sharply restrained but noisy slap on the bare bottom, a spanking administered with a threatening tree branch called a "switch," or perhaps the intended muffled, mumbling, fumbled struggle of taking off "the belt" and belatedly missing to catch one's truly frightened, shrieking objective.

One's father understood the philosophy of "spare the rod and spoil the child," which was epitomized within the grandfather's era. An "at arm's length" parental bearing was prevalent among silent, repressed fathers, and it is naturally embodied to me by Grandfather Grant, whether this perception is fair to his memory or not. He represented family aloofness and nobility, even if possibly only by default. His place and purpose in the family were palatable particularly to a wee wide-eyed and contemplative lad.

Adults strangely seemed to consider, as you got to know them better, that individual differences and extraordinary achievements were almost always patently superfluous, big-headed, or selfish at the core. A purely rational or psychological understanding of human behavior was stigmatized as secular and judged necessary only for the faithless, godless, and sacrilegious. A secular psychology was neither known nor comprehensible to adults in the generation of our overworked, poverty-stricken, undereducated, trusting, honest, under-appreciated, overtly economically and socially slighted, and gladly taciturn grandparents.

These adults were, nonetheless, godlike to a young boy or girl in the 1940s and '50s. Honesty was as certain an entity in the working-class community as the threat of disproportionate and overreactive policing is now. Trust between like-minded adults was a golden rule long before the naïveté and unawareness of common citizens were unsympathetically exposed and distrust of the ordinary became common given governmental abuses of power in the 1960s and '70s. A grown man's word was much of his currency in my grandparents' day, and it was simultaneously assumed that only the children could not be trusted because they were naturally unpredictable and unreliable due to immaturity or lack of education.

A self-taught farm mechanic like Howard Grant and an artist like his younger brother Corwin shared a common sense of the social morality of the day in spite of other differences. At that time, though, the clergymen were the most important authorities. In the family, parents referenced the local pastor more than all other professional powers, including the doctor, policeman, teacher, and judge, who were thought to be only developing authorities. Now all the professions are as ubiquitous as the church, or more so, and they compete for ultimate devotion and knowledge as at no other time in history.

There was a lot to think over and try to put into words after an actual encounter with grown-ups like Granddad. Loyalty to each other and tacit faith in common social values were assumed at face value and taken very much for granted. Much was left unsaid between individuals or generations, but goodwill and a general brotherhood were rightly assumed as the proper posturing. Unlike today, most men were good followers, not merely frustrated leaders with no followers. If typical people could not be good leaders in many instances, there were many people who were proud to be simple, reliable, and trustworthy followers.

Grant men and women conscientiously exhibited the quiet and devoted characteristics of faith, trustworthiness, reliability, humble competence, and a wide-ranging working-class confidence over all. Emoting and social liberalism were uncharacteristic of this strong, organized, geared-up and ready tribe. People were to be treated alike as long as no trust was broken. There was little understanding or tolerance of creativity or diversity as there is now.

In less contemporary times, gender roles and responsibilities were sharply divided and defined between boy and girl, man and women. The typical man was a rigid breadwinner. The typical woman was a stay-at-home mother, competent cook, and homemaker. Assumption of gender-appropriate, gender-distinct interests and roles was endemic. Poetry was coldheartedly discouraged in the teaching and upbringing of the boys. Participation in sports was unsympathetically discouraged among the girls.

The result was each child's awareness of his or her limited stature and the importance of proving his or her worth through conformity and hard work. The typical family product was, before the 1960s, a sort of stoic mechanistic problem solver who responded to social and cultural issues as they devolved in the local arena. Challenges, of which there were certainly always many, were mostly shaped in the long run by the only available jobs and a limited local economy.

Occupations at the bleeding edge of the Industrial Revolution commonly provided a new source of income for many hardworking men. This climate raised family income by allowing men to work for entrepreneurs. Many men were performing and supervising at home on the farm and laboring or supervising as foremen in "real" jobs that came from capitalists outside the influence of the family farm.

In Granddaddy's boyhood, the typical family home in America was a homestead. This multigenerational family centered place of birth was commonly encapsulated within tens of acres of open spaces composed of ponds, streams, fields, and forests. Homesteads belonged to a free, strong, independent people. Heads of households seldom answered to anyone but their own consciences or the likeminded. Men might listen to their wives and siblings but make all final decisions for the family, at least in public.

It was even commonly said that, "Children should be seen and not heard." And the children quickly assumed dutiful roles within their comparatively isolated family structures. Schooling didn't even begin until children were six years of age. It often ended after the fourth grade, when the child was ten or eleven years of age, as was the case for my maternal grandfather, Tom Young. The next generation, represented to me by Mother, graduated high school. College graduation exalted our generation.

The unrestricted land on the homestead also excited and reinforced a sense of liberty and the spirit of exploration. The mark of success was a homestead that was life sustaining and independent even in the education of children.

Youngsters of all ages typically dwelled with parents and any surviving grandparents under the common roof. This style of living went all the way back to the days of the colony. Labor on the farm was shared among all and parceled out to each family member according to age, gender, and the uncanny propensity to take on any task left shunned, misunderstood, or abandoned by any of the others. The family encouraged this behavior since it created a needed hierarchy that automatically managed the contrasting roles of children and adults. The oldest children often chose the responsibility of being the leaders, middle children often became the mediators and negotiators, and the smallest, or the children considered weakest or weirdest in the family, becoming the self-acknowledged purveyors of sarcasm, self-ridicule, and insult, the alienated lackadaisical family cynics.

My great-grandfather Louis Dunham Grant (1859–1934) was the last boy to be born on our original Tahan Grant homestead in Wapping, the northern section of East Windsor. His father, Norman Owen Grant (1831–1900), lived on the family farm there like everyone before him, but he eventually developed secondary interests and talents and consequently moved away to live in West Hartford. As infamous as Norman became to the Tahan branch of the family, in a parallel lifetime, his cousin Ulysses S. Grant was becoming genuinely famous for all the proper reasons.

Norman Owen Grant and Mariah Dunham of Mansfield married and had two children on the farm in East Windsor. These disadvantaged children grew up to become Great-Grandfather Louis and his sister, Josephine. After a decade of marriage, the restless, temperamental, and selfish Norman Owen began to find the endless chores of farming too boring. Even with the help of lovely Mariah and two children, he wanted a more thought-provoking, active purpose in life than that of farming.

N. O. Grant apparently believed he was born suitable for more inspiring distinctions and left the farming life behind to become a schoolteacher about the time of the Civil War. On this career path, he met a young Irish immigrant woman, abruptly abandoned the Grant family homestead as well as Mariah, Louie, and Jo, and made a new life for himself and his young bride and teaching colleague across the Connecticut River in the town of West Hartford.

Mariah eventually moved with the two children to live with her parents in Mansfield. Some time later, she left temporary accommodations there, moving to the nearby city of Manchester to live permanently in a big white colonial house at 22 Pine Hill Road, within walking range of North Main Street and the local Methodist and Congregational churches, non-farm jobs, and better suburban public schools.

Having adjusted to the new experiences of small-city life, Great-Granddad Louis married a Manchester girl who lived on Hudson Street. He wed Emogene Hudson (1863–1951) on June 1, 1885. By 1905, their home in Manchester was the place of birth of nine brothers and sisters. Six of these children were living when Grandfather was a young man. Helen, Gertrude, Maude, Howard, Corwin, and the youngest of the children, Dorothy, were among the first generation of Grants to be raised in the Silk City, or the City of Village Charm, as Manchester is called now. The kids were among the first Americans obtaining schooling and experience in the fast-developing non-farm occupations of the Industrial Revolution.

Helen's daughter Marilyn Shead Peterson wrote the following letter about our great-grandparents Louis and Emogene. I obtained a copy of this message as a gift from cousin Susan Shead when she helped gather Grant family information many years ago at the Windsor Historical Society. At the time it was previously unknown to either of us … our relationships to Ulysses S. Grant, and our many other common ancestors.

Aunt Marilyn wrote:

Grandma Grant (Emogene) was a very gentle, loving and very hard working woman. She was a wonderful cook—always made cookies for us kids and when I think of her I always remember her fondly. One evening she and I went to a minstrel show that Mom was in and I can remember walking home to spend the night at her house. I was very young then but I was very proud to finally be a "big" girl. I think perhaps Mom sang "Um-m, Um-m, Um-m, Would You Like to Take A Walk?" Anyway, that's always been one of my favorite songs.

I can remember coming to Woodstock with Mom, Dad, Grandma, Gramps, Donnie and even Billy as a tiny one. The roads weren't as good then or the cars either, but we'd start early. Mom would pack a picnic lunch to eat someplace along the way and by the time we got home to Manchester at night it would be quite late. And when we moved to Woodstock in the early days everyone would come for a day long visit and then when we had the Duck Pond we'd spend the day down there. It was fun. But, unfortunately, we didn't get together often enough. It seemed a long way to go in those days. I still have a long string of red glass beads that Grandma used to let me dress up in. I wonder if I was supposed to give them back?

Grandpa Grant, as I remember him, was a scholarly man. He loved to read and I remember every day he'd go to the Park in Manchester for a little jug of fresh spring water. He stayed with Mom and us kids at night for several weeks while my Dad (Edgar) was in Woodstock settling the details

about buying his trucking business. Donald was sick at that time and we were quarantined. I remember we had big red signs on our doors and no one was supposed to come in or go out. I had to stay home from school too. Scarlet Fever was very serious and Donnie was very sick.

Grandpa (Louie) couldn't believe that I didn't read the newspaper. As I recall he'd always offer me the love-story section. It was a continuous story every day. And although I did my best I couldn't read that story at all. I think we were struggling with Dick, Jane and Spot at school. He finally gave up and gave me the funny papers instead—I looked at the pictures anyway. And that started my interest in reading. He tried to teach dominoes but he didn't like me to count on my fingers so that didn't go over very well either. He was very proud of his Cousin, General Grant. Uncle Corwin can tell you about that, I'm sure. Mom said we shouldn't brag too much about him because he was an alcoholic and in those days it wasn't considered a disease—it was a disgrace, even if you did wonderful things. And Grandma's relative, Henry Hudson, was very distant.

Gramp's father was supposed to have been a wealthy man who remarried a younger woman. We didn't talk about these things but Mom and her family had lively discussions about first cousins and cousins once removed. Please try to get to see Uncle Corwin. He's got a wonderful memory still and would be so pleased that you are interested. When I think of Mom's family I always think of a lively, loving and interested family group. I wanted to be as wonderful an Aunt to my nieces and nephews as they were to me.

Aunt Helen's brother was our grandfather. Howard Grant became a young tractor mechanic because for the first time machines were a source of reliable income. He was the first of the family to be raised around machines rather than around the ubiquitous sundry farm animals that farmers exploited for the sake of their productivity. Howard soon found an opportunity for significant full-time employment as a machinist and rifle assembler during World War I in Bridgeport. After this episode of wartime employment, and for most of his adult life, he was making, repairing, maintaining, or operating machinery as a millwright in local Manchester business enterprises, including employers at the Bon Ami soap factory and the Sealtest dairy.

He lived in Bridgeport, Connecticut, during the First World War for more than a year but returned to Manchester in 1918. His generation completed the transition from independent family farming to routine days of factory-floor work all over the country. Machines were slowly but surely replacing beasts of burden for the first time in history, and the Industrial Revolution was certainly changing life on Manchester city streets.

Howard was another eldest son. He was composed, self-assured, patient, precise, and thorough in his work. He became a self-disciplined, dependable worker for several serial company capitalists who were willing to offer hourly wages for the "right man." He had greatly needed skills peculiar to the industrial era that he was, for all apparent intents and purposes, born to build upon steadily as a hardworking man and as a quick learner.

Tool assiduousness was inherited, by me. Instinctively sensing both the importance of my grandfather's old tools and a prime opportunity for myself as the first and eldest grandson, I selfishly (but not shamelessly) gained control of the tools that granddad and dad had used over the years prior to my birth. Grandfather was dead and gone by then, and my father was a full-time tool designer, preoccupied thirtyish year old college student, and new homeowner. I cornered and collected the antique wrenches, handsaws, hammers, and screwdrivers for my own childhood toolbox. Along with these long-cherished tools came the inspired acumen to effectively and satisfyingly employ them around the house. An even-headed awareness of entitlement, a willingness to work, and an intense affection for granddad steadily made me more capable of making and repairing many wonderful things with these family tools. Now I think of this windfall as akin to the gift of a chemistry lab implement collection to an aspiring young scientist. I simply wanted to be more grown-up and to be recognized as a valued, self-sufficient member of the family. I understood nothing about how oppositional that apparently seemed then to dad.

Robert ultimately applied his socially perceptive, analytical mind toward effective and efficient methods for adult mental health counseling in a hospital setting. Steven became a legal counselor and a municipal judge in Brooklyn, and suburban New York. Neither came to know, as I did, about the tacit dignity inherent in corporal work that granddad had done all of his life.

Naturally, accomplishing some long-term gains in life expectancy and quality of life was worthy side effects of my higher level of physical work and exercise. Though older than my brothers by five years, and twelve years respectively, I have secured for myself a high quality of life and a healthy longevity by obtaining and maintaining the habit of routine physical exercise. I gained this self-sustaining natural habit while I was independently painting the interiors and exteriors of houses for income during adolescence and my college years.

Our grandfather's brother, Corwin, was socially and emotionally vulnerable but also kind, empathetic, respectful, and reserved. He became a graphic artist, by which occupation he supported an independent wifeless and childless life that included sign-painting services, and employment with the Cheney Fabric Mills of Manchester. I recall dad telling me that his mother had dated Corwin first. She hadn't even known Howard, before Corwin introduced them. Then they started dating.

There is little doubt as to why she came to favor the quiet, strong, industrious Howard Grant over our favorite younger uncle. Howard already had a "real job" that provided steady income. He had the kind of proven, reliable work ethic that all real employers—and ladies—wanted at that time. This made all the difference in the world for Corwin's prospects in our life.

Corwin received some sympathy, compensation, and consolation through inside help getting a job at the silk mill. Grandmother's father, Thomas Noble, worked as a wet-velvet finisher in the Cheney fabric mills after his immigration from Northern Ireland and Scotland to Manchester in 1903. He left Ireland for training in Scotland after his marriage to my great-grandmother Isabella Crocket. Feeling sorry for Corwin and generally sensitive to the general livelihood of the Grant family, he put in a good word or two for his kinesthetically and aesthetically gifted but jilted young artistic acquaintance.

Many years later, Corwin was answering questions for his three nephews at the Manchester hospital where he had been admitted for weakness of the heart. Robert, Steven, and I were together, visiting. He must have answered at least a dozen questions in detail that day about his life and experiences. When asked what our granddad was like as a brother, Corwin abruptly stopped answering our questions, stared off vacantly, and said nothing more that day about life and relations. Sadly, this was the last time we saw him alive, and I regret that he had no words he could use to describe to us the life of our granddad, Howard L. Grant, Sr.

In his young adulthood, my great-granddad Tom Noble immigrated from Northern Ireland to Scotland to master a trade in the woolen industry, and within a couple of years, a little after the turn of the twentieth century, he left Kilsyth, Stirlingshire, Scotland, with his young wife and my grandmother Rebecca. Rebecca had been born in Northern Ireland. In America, she and her parents, along with siblings John, Alex, and Lizzie, first lived at 31 North Elm Street, Manchester, in a house that was less than a five-hundred-yard walk for Tom to the job at the Cheney Mills. This initial factory residence for newcomers was soon inadequate for their growing family, so the Nobles moved to 21 Wadsworth Street, a large two-family, two-story colonial, which was about a mile away from the mill if you walked diagonally through the town park. Otherwise, Tom's walk down Main Street to Hartford Road and to his job would have taken almost an hour without any horse or wagon.

Over the first three centuries in America, the land surrounding old homesteads was used less and less exclusively for farming by each successive generation. Increasingly, the land was sold to industry or to independent contractors who constructed factories or built smaller homes for much smaller families until these modern residences surrounded almost all of the old larger, traditional farmhouses on all sides.

The windfalls of cash raised from selling these large private parcels of land, either all at once or a little at a time, were increasingly used by parents and grandparents to pay for college educations and aspirations of mastering different disciplines or setting out in many other lifestyles other than farming. Property ownership was the raw fuel for American dreams. Property was often given away to successive generations through inheritances, but as large expanses of land appreciated in value, that land became a source of prosperity and freedom for the final titleholders.

Visible evidence of the long, graceful fields of rye and endless forests being subdivided and sold as a contiguous series of smaller lots was painfully untraditional, quite conspicuously greedy, and unfortunately common in many suburban towns in Connecticut when I was a boy about sixty years ago. By the time our parents' generation needed land for homes, the typical house was only about eight to twelve-hundred square feet and built for a theoretically ideal family of four: father, mother, son, and daughter. During this modern time, grandparents also often bought or rented a small home nearby and became unpaid assistants for childcare, particularly when it became possible for both parents to bring home a paycheck. Work outside the home became necessary to keep a non-farm, middle-class lifestyle possible for many.

My great-grandfather Louis Dunham Grant was a little shorter and more muscular than the young sons of the present generation, who averaged almost six feet in height as adults. Though typically about five feet six inches in height, fully grown Grant men from Tahan Grant's branch were muscular and stocky, due perhaps to experiences demanding more physical labor at an early age. The physical health of more than a couple generations was undermined by mandatory school experiences with few physical activities allowed in direct comparison to the rapidly disappearing farm lifestyle. There was an hour of recess every school day, but gym was scheduled for only one or two thirty-minute classes a week, if any. Children who walked to school and home again every day may also have walked home for lunch and missed recess play until town-wide school consolidations of school campuses took place and most students were bused to centralized locations by the 1960s. Most families had only one car, if any, up to the early '60s.

It really wasn't until after World War II that universal public education for children even began to be a crucial concern. As one of the oldest members of the baby boom generation, I was given grades based on how much I was willing to intellectually consume through rote memorization of lots of pointless factual material. Teachers failed to facilitate learning in a context that was meaningful for a boy like me. From the underdeveloped individual perspective of a kid, it was difficult to understand just how useful learning could be. Before computers were used in the classroom, a boy or girl was expected to learn what adults thought was important in a rigid step-by-step manner. A youngster who was prepared properly could readily compartmentalize and develop his interests in a concrete and sequential way. These students could do better than those who found school stifling, unnatural, and useless. The repetitious mastery of sequential factual material in grades one through eight, including much of the material in most important subjects, reading, writing, and arithmetic, was considered modern pedagogy. Broadly supported by teachers and parents, the curriculum simply aimed at the basic skills for the sake of conformity, or mastery, from well into the late mid-twentieth century. Adults could barely begin to imagine childhood developmental needs and interests, let alone clarify specific worthwhile learning targets. As the professions of education and psychology developed in this period, teaching promised to change for the better. Sadly, most teachers were blind to the independent inquisitive mind and the brain-based attributes of the learning process until the late 1960s and '70s, when I was in graduate school. Certainly many students of my generation and those before it never realized the joys of lifelong liberal arts and science learning unless they also had exposure to higher education.

Until the fifth grade, I concentrated mostly on daydreaming. I daydreamed about the endless process of discovery in the joyful woods and fields near my parents' small garrison-style colonial at 660 Forbes Street in East Hartford. I daydreamed about anything outside and beyond the big, newly constructed brick building that adults arranged to keep children in all day long. On rainy days, or in the winter, the shelter was warm and comfortable, but on sunny days in the spring and fall, school was full of angst.

The Sunset Ridge Elementary School was constructed just after the Second World War and had been open for only four years when I was sent off from home at about five years of age to go there. The social aspects of schooling were normally benign and beneficial, as a natural form of interaction of like-minded children actually occurred, excepting the competition for severely limited resources like the blocks you needed to complete a castle in kindergarten or the undisturbed use of a crayon in any hue other than black.

In those times, public school prioritized personal thinking, exploration, discovery, and creativity in the classroom only as underwhelming afterthoughts until the seventh or eighth grade, when some projects and independent studies were introduced. Art and music activities slowly evolved from the classes of a few part-time, itinerant teachers who taught "specials." These teachers were always the most inspiring and ironically the most marginalized by the school system, according to my perspective then. They had no classrooms because of very limited educational resources in general, and in particular for elementary arts and sciences. These bold teachers attracted my attention. They unapologetically pushed their noisy, tall, and shaky carts to and from other teachers' classrooms down the long halls of the school. You could hear them coming and going at thirty-minute intervals all week long but could only see them in person once a week.

It was due to one of these valiant teachers that I learned to read books for pleasure. A reading specialist was the first to give Mother advice on what books I could read to learn that reading is a source of endless learning and fun. This worked really well.

Due to the general inadequacy of arts and science in the curriculum, I slowly developed a preference for the relief and development that books brought psychologically. Individual sensitivity, creativity, and theoretical thought were not endorsed actively at that elementary school level. Worse yet, parents often discouraged inquisitiveness and independent research as quite useless and unwelcome for the purposes of schooling. Anything worth inventing or doing had already been done quite well enough, it seemed. I naturally defaulted to the belief that every subject worth pursuing was already the best it would ever be. It was impossible to perceive then that every fact and method of understanding was really quite new and would likely be short-lived.

By any standard, I was certainly cured of persistent daydreaming before I entered the fifth grade. Mrs. Symington was not a new teacher or a terribly old one but someone who surely had taught the fourth grade with natural tranquility, joy, and composure in her heart all through World War II. She was very kind and beautiful in a mature, maternal manner, more nearly similar to a loving grandparent than to anyone else. Other than the fact that she had persistently tried to redirect my attention to the subject at hand, I never expected any really serious consequences to issue from this firm, fair, and gentlewoman.

I would consistently lapse into daydreaming after a respectable initial period of struggling to follow along with every subject being presented in the classroom page by page. This was specifically true with group reading out loud because I didn't want to embarrass Mrs. Symington. She was, in my thoroughly considered assessment, the type of person who would freely allow for individual differences among children and could see a child's greater potential where others might simply perceive indolence. So I recall reasoning that I could get away with less than an earnest and vigorous concentration in school on many subjects. I loved Mrs. Symington because she was attentive and respectful to me as a person and had, I lovingly thought, not a mean bone in her body toward her classroom of kids. The only slightly annoying instructional characteristic she exhibited was her ability to catch me daydreaming persistently throughout the entire fourth-grade year.

My school respected the tradition of announcing promotions to the next grade level in the last hour of the last day of school each year. The fourth grade was no exception, and students actually enjoyed the suspense and surprise of finding out their assignments for the following year and celebrating among themselves even before their parents were told the news. In an instant, we would quickly revel in our excitement at formally being fifth graders, at last.

At only ten years of age, I believed it still wasn't really natural to worry about academic competency and an individual scholarly repute. Being a satisfactory or solid *C* student was good enough, even though I had the potential to do the work to obtain better-than-average grades or maybe even achieve excellence with an intense and devoted commitment to some subjects.

But this routine last minute school-wide announcement, delivered by the principal over the public address system, began ever so slowly to arouse in me unusual discomfort. Still, I good-naturedly waited for my name to be called and to be linked with a terrific fifth-grade teacher. I still consciously demonstrated no fear and shrugged off the obvious mistake that had been made when my name was still not announced as they moved on from classmates' surnames beginning with the letter *G* to those beginning with *H* and so on. The rotating guile and guilt of being, at all these critical junctures, the most attentive student in the classroom was indigestible.

Out of my entire classroom of thirty-two children, my raised hand was the first to get Mrs. Symington's attention. She was, God bless her heart, sincerely concerned and willing to help me that very minute! Her cool-headed kindness and customary magnanimity were commensurate with the destructive intensity of my heated distress and embarrassment. Astonished, she said, "Tommy, it must be all just a big mistake! *Go to the office immediately and tell Miss Leahy* [the school principal] about it."

In those postwar school days, no kid in his right mind wanted to go down to the principal's office. But for this breathtaking problem and purpose, I thought it was very important for me to step up for sure.

After ignoring me for what seemed like another whole school year, Miss Leahy finally looked up over the top of her reading glasses, stared directly at me through the open door from her office desk, and asked, "Tommy, why are *you* here?" Red-faced and sweating profusely, I awkwardly and guardedly stood at her office door to tell her about the big mistake, feeling less welcome than the puddle that I remember always collected in the front doorway of the Sunset Ridge School, just outside the principal's office, after a hard rain.

Fortunately, she quickly agreed; she had made an awfully big mistake. She looked at a paper on her desk for a very long time and finally produced the announcement that I remember word for word: "You are promoted to the fifth grade, and your teacher will be Ms. McCluskie.

Graciously accepting what I perceived as an absolutely sincere apology, I backed out her office door and enthusiastically went back to inform my lovable fourth-grade teacher of the wonderful news! One was not allowed to run or skip in the halls, but that day was an exception for me!

I'm sure Mrs. Symington felt that she earned her pay that day. Certainly ever since that momentous day I have felt a strong internalized drive and accurate sense of direction as a learner. From that significant experience, I honestly was ready for the fifth grade like no other.

While I progressed through the more advanced grade levels, the "mistake" never occurred again, and I'm sure that the principal and Mrs. Symington heard about my improved attention and aptitude when they talked to my fifth-grade teacher. The significant event, instilled a me a strong belief in my personal responsibility for life-long learning.

As fate would have it, I happened to read Mrs. Symington's obituary about forty-five years later, and found that she had taught the fourth grade for more than thirty-five years and had enjoyed retirement with her husband, Dr. Thomas Symington, MD, for another considerable period of time. Perhaps at some point in her long career, a paper written by me about my favorite teacher had appeared in her school mailbox. I hope so, because even though it wasn't very convenient, or even possible to tell her in person, I always recalled her as my favorite teacher. I always will believe that I owed her that special, out-of-the-ordinary recognition.

CHAPTER 18

The River Gods

Ebenezer Grant's Higher Education,
East Windsor Commerce, and the World Economy

GRANT FAMILY ANCESTORS WERE STILL only two or three provincial
generations of parents, brothers, sisters, and many cousins then, before the Revolution, but all were direct descendants of Mathew Grant.
Samuel, the firstborn son, was first in the family to build a home across
the Great River at a site to the east of Windsor. The needs of industry
and the prosperity of Windsor encouraged several more of the second
and third generations of Dorchester families to live, work, and create a
second ecclesiastical society, building a church for worship there. The
devoted could now move permanently across the Great River to the east
and south of Windsor, where they would find free acres of land for grazing livestock, along with good soil for the farming of grains like wheat
and corn and for the cultivation of broadleaf tobacco, which would lead
to extraordinary increases in New England export trading with the existing worldwide network of trading companies.

By the turn of the eighteenth century, small-scale ships that were
sufficiently maneuverable on the river were being built specifically
for services connecting emerging colonial commerce between the

communities of Windsor, Hartford, Wethersfield, and Middletown on the west bank and East Windsor, Glastonbury, and Portland on the east-bank, with the West Indies trade serving as a ready hub of international enterprise. A growing fleet of new two-mast schooners of 120 feet in length, similar to the early nineteenth-century *Amistad*, could navigate the Connecticut River as far north as Windsor and be suitable for coastal shipping as far south as Cuba and the Caribbean. The east-side sawmill at the mouth of the Scantic River, which was developed and operated by both the Samuel Grants, father and son, was the site for many original aspects of the emerging Connecticut Colony shipbuilding industry.

There were as many as four thousand English settlers living in Connecticut Colony by 1670 in Mathew Grant's parallel moment of Windsor parish tenure. Samuel and other direct descendants were to benefit socially and financially from their vital association with the profitable network of craftsmen that was responsible for creating the legacy of early American colonial furniture such as the Windsor chair, for the design and construction of authentic colonial homes in the river valley and, perhaps above all, for the trading ships constructed specifically for the Connecticut Colony economy.

The Samuel Grant family worked and prospered from their East Windsor Hill farm on the busy north-to-south Boston Post Road. That well-travelled road ran past Rye Street in Wapping, where the enterprising Tahan, Jr., family quietly farmed many acres and cultivated waves of rye that blew in the winds. At the next corner, the Post Road turned sharply left from Samuel Jr.'s land and continued south past Samuel's farm, running parallel to the river, toward Hartford. Land routes paralleled the river toward the simultaneously and rapidly developing economies of Hartford, Wethersfield, Middletown, and New Haven. Beyond these Connecticut River towns, south along the Atlantic coast, was New York, a frenetic and prosperous Dutch trading colony.

Two sons of Samuel, Jr., Noah and Ebenezer Grant, were born in 1694 and 1706 respectively at East Windsor Hill. The twelve years between them became a much larger and more pronounced difference as each went along a different developmental pathway and made divergent choices. As they grew up, though, both boys were thoroughly exposed to farming, carpentry, and sundry other trade skills. The boys learned by working at the family enterprise next to their father and their revered grandfather Mathew Grant and through projects and temporary apprenticeships with physically and mentally disciplined neighbors and skilled business acquaintances.

As adolescents, Noah and Ebenezer also helped manage customer care and services at their father and grandfather's sawmill and became capable carpenters for the soon-to-be-built parish church and the first large colonial homes within the community of East Windsor and the Connecticut River Valley at large. They mastered the necessary trades to guarantee a prosperous future for the colony.

Noah and Ebenezer's great-granddad Mathew had retired from public and ecclesiastical administration in Windsor after thirty years of honest service to the town of Windsor and the First Church of Windsor. So when Noah had a suitable opportunity, he took advantage of his good luck to make a move, as his grandfather had done, to what was to become a new settlement in Tolland. By the time of the move, Mathew had already passed away thirteen years before, but the memory of the legendary man was still keen in the minds of all. He would have blessed the opportunity to get in on the ground floor of an adventure like this one, or so Noah thought. After all, the old predecessor's wisdom had embraced establishing himself early, mastering a meaningful state of affairs in a new community, and growing upright, respected, and progressive through the experience. It was simple to see that Noah's great-grandfather's dedication and persistence had made him socially viable, durable, and secure.

This was the beginning of something big and worthy of the idealistic Noah Grant, he thought. He felt that he was strong, internally motivated, and as eager as anyone to make something from his hearty potential. He was keyed up to be useful, especially given the significant reputations of the family members whom he intensely desired to impress. He was, after all, the eldest of his siblings and could point the way for Ebenezer and the others by purposeful living, just as his father, granddad, and great-grandfather had already done within recent memory.

Noah was influenced by where the successful family experience had been. The younger brother was looking to where the potential future would likely be.

Noah had explored and fallen in love with the high ground in Tolland, with its awesome views of continuous forest as far as the eye could see to the east. He reasoned that his sharp younger brother, Ebenezer, and several dependable cousins could help him build a great house at the attractive spot. He would settle in, marry his sweetheart, and raise sons and daughters to help on the farm and around his new beautiful home, as everyone else in the family had dreamed of doing before him.

Noah was sure that his plans would be difficult but convinced himself that they would work out well over a long enough time. He also very much needed to get a suitable distance away from the routine at the sawmill and to do what God had inspired and prepared him all along to uniquely do.

Noah's homestead was twenty miles farther east of Windsor, with an expansive treetop view of the surrounding countryside. Soon enough, after his permanent arrival, the road to his farm was dubbed Grant Hill Road by an ad hoc group of neighbors, the local parish citizens and friends.

By 1720, the nearby turnpike at Tolland stretched seventy-five miles to Boston in the east and eighty-three miles to Albany, New York, in the west. Noah knew that the twenty miles from Hartford was an inconvenient but reasonable distance to the farmer's market if one used this fast toll road for transportation with a couple of horses and a good family wagon. This turnpike was good enough to allow a farmer to reach Hartford in a little less than a day, sell produce, have a little fun in the city with farming friends, and return the next day to the farm. The new turnpike thus strategically enhanced Connecticut's position as the pivotal center of New England trade and commerce over land and would within about five decades rightly earn Connecticut the reputation and title of "the Provision State" during and after the Revolutionary War.

The dilapidated old house that had been the home of the Grants of Tolland for three generations was restored by a builder from South Windsor in 1986, more than two hundred years after the life of Noah. Incredibly, the Sunderland Company specialized in duplicating period structures utilizing the original skills and salvaged tools of the building trades from the colonial period. The Tolland house was recognized during the renovation work for being the birthplace of Noah Grant, the great-grandfather of President Grant. This deteriorating early wooden structure had stood abandoned for many years and was perhaps always a raw reminder of the not-so-glorious decline of Ulysses Grant's family fortunes in just two or three generations following the Revolutionary War. Though most likely virtually free for the taking at one time, the rocky land in Tolland was notoriously difficult for families and farms to prosper on so many years ago. Those venturing there had little but hard times and disappointment to pass on to heirs.

The 1725 Noah Grant House, Tolland, Circa 1987

Noah, Jr., the great-grandfather of Ulysses. S. Grant and the son born in the Tolland house became the figure whom the history-minded Sunderland Company recalled in all the publicity for their considerate, careful restoration work on the grand house.

I was an excited eyewitness to the outstanding quality of their restoration work and the replication of the original woodworking specifically because I made the visit to the Sunderland Company workshop in 1986. A large barn had been upgraded to workrooms that reminded me of New England antiquity in detail. Everywhere I looked, there were craftsmen working on projects with authentic tools and methods of the seventeenth and eighteenth centuries. The experience made me envious of the pleasure generated by the hours of labor it took to make an authentic handcrafted window or door. I also wondered who could afford such handmade perfection given the wages of craftsmen in mid-twentieth-century America. I concluded that it was a labor of love and that everyone involved would lose money on the magnificent project. But I thoroughly felt the pain of not possessing enough time, talent, experience, or money to restore a house as this great company would. This disappointment made me think of how much Noah Grant had experienced and ponder the true wealth of any of our lives, no matter how it's measured. It is perhaps not how long we live or how few years we have to make our mark but the joy of meaningful vision that makes a difference. When hindsight is twenty-twenty, it is possible to perceive the brightness of a single being among the family circumstances, including his or her aspirations and life skills and the afterglow of his reach.

I am aware of only one other source that has recognized and recalled properly the lives of Grant family members and the sequence of Noah Grant's experiences in Tolland. This book is *The Grant Family* by Arthur Hastings Grant, published in 1898. This book lists the hundreds of parents, siblings, and cousins born into the Grant family up to its publication.

In this more current rendition of family relations, the most significant relationships are treated in brief biographical sketches. This method may illuminate further Grant family legacies and myths, particularly in the numinous complex surrounding Noah Grant. For instance, the second Noah Grant became the human historical nexus between two presidential families due to his marriage to Susannah Delano on November 5, 1746, which marked the phenomenal linkage of two future American war-era presidents, Ulysses S. Grant and president Franklin Delano Roosevelt.

Mr. Sunderland, owner of Sunderland Company, hadn't been aware that the great-grandfather of Ulysses S. Grant had a father of the same name. He didn't know that the first Noah was the one who had actually built the house he intended to reconstruct or that the forgotten Noah was the grandson of the family progenitor, Mathew Grant. I was pleased to provide a live, in-person commentary on the essential points of the story to a man I now so totally admired, the master builder Mr. Sunderland.

The 1725 Noah Grant House, Circa 1987

This first Noah Grant had left East Windsor to follow his own dreams in Tolland while Samuel Grant, Jr., was soon successful in getting his younger son, Ebenezer, into college at Yale in New Haven. Prospects could not have been brighter for this young man's future, but not so much can be said for the eldest son. Ebenezer was the one to make the best of Samuel's existing station in synchrony with Connecticut River Valley culture. Noah chose a path that held fewer rewarding circumstances.

Noah was completely engrossed in physical work as a farmer and carpenter during the years in which Ebenezer quietly and unceremoniously earned a higher education. During both their lifetimes, the father of Noah and Ebenezer was turning everything he touched into good fortune at East Windsor Hill. Even late in the eighth decade of a long life, his physical labor and the rapid growth of local commerce would sustain this busy East Windsor developer, Samuel Grant Jr.

In stark comparison to East Windsor, Tolland proved isolated and difficult, even perhaps a totally depressing place for Sam's eldest son Noah. Subsistence farming with few or no surplus goods to bring to market offered few worldly satisfactions for a man in his thirties who expected much more from life while observing, certainly with some misgivings, his fully socially and commercially occupied and resoundingly successful father and his younger brother Ebenezer. Sadly, Noah died in the year 1727, at the age of only thirty-three, when Noah Jr. was a boy just nine years of age.

The French and Indian War ameliorated Noah Jr.'s severe feelings of uselessness and boredom on the remote farm. The aphorisms that pertained to Noah's mordant situation aptly enough were "like father, like son," and "the apple doesn't fall far from the tree."

Perhaps for the appeal of pleasant companionship and for badly needed help with the farm, Noah Grant Jr. introduced himself to an attractive young woman who attended the new Congregational church located at the Coventry end of Grant Hill Road. Following courtship and marriage, the couple worked the Grant Hill Road farm together awhile before this uneasy and self-assured young man saw it necessary to enlist in the English army in 1754. Noah thought to enhance his overall worldly experiences and augment his farm income with benefits for his wife and children through the attractive promised military pension after the war.

Unfortunately, his decision to join the struggle against the invading French Canadians and insurgent Mohawks was nothing less than the personal catastrophe he feared the most. In less than two years, he was assumed dead, the result of scouting in the mountains and wilderness surrounding Fort Ticonderoga in New York. In the same conflict with their enemy, his brave brother Solomon was also killed fighting for the security of the not too distant home in Connecticut.

At home, Noah's pregnant wife, helped by family, neighbors, and charity from the local church, worked to help make life on the Tolland family farm continue without the captain. She did this until her son, the third Noah, was strong and experienced enough to do most of the farm labor. When Suzanna Delano went to Coventry to assist her elderly parents, an opportunity presented itself, and she married a widowed member of the Congregational church, Mr. Buell, who owned a farm there, and the two of them raised a family, providing Noah with several half brothers and sisters.

Finally, the third Noah Grant chose to escape the burden of his grandfather's initial decision to leave prosperous East Windsor. Shortly after serving a sentence in a Connecticut debtors prison for failing to pay creditors, bankrupted and discontented, he abandoned the farm and migrated many miles from Connecticut. He passed through Pennsylvania and then Kentucky, where he remarried. He ended his migration, staying put in what would be the future state of Ohio but was the Western Reserve of Connecticut at the time.

No colonial record has been found to officially substantiate the distinct impression, given to others by the third Noah himself, of his Revolutionary War service. Unlike most of his contemporaries from Connecticut, he received no military pension for service to his country.

Unlike Nathan Hale of Coventry, he was never caught or hanged for espionage against the king of England. Later in life, he sadly admitted that he had had unusually bad luck obtaining and preserving worldly goods; neither could he, apparently, even obtain recognition for his intensely exhibited patriot views. The third Noah was something of an unfortunate, voluble jingoist; he was also the improvident father of Jesse Root Grant.

In the more prosperous position at East Windsor Hill, the other male heir of Sam, Jr., Ebenezer Grant, surveyed most of South Windsor and was a distinguished clerk, from 1733 to 1767, of the Second Ecclesiastical Society, as well as sheriff and selectman between 1776 and 1781. Throughout these years, he was always a sharply appointed, plucky, and happy contrast to his much younger grandnephew, the third Noah Grant.

Ebenezer Grant added a shipbuilding enterprise to the fine family timber-milling business at the mouth of the Scantic River in East Windsor. This enterprise further facilitated and promoted his interests in shipping with river towns, such as Glastonbury, to accommodate the growth of New England commerce overall. Warehouses were built on both sides of the Great River in towns like Middletown, Wethersfield, Glastonbury, Hartford, and Windsor as the river towns continued to prosper up to the Revolution. Ebenezer and his sons maintained privileged roles in it all. His socially delightful daughter Anne married the Wethersfield minister John Marsh on December 6, 1775. An account book kept by Ebenezer and his son Roswell lists expensive furniture made in the East Windsor shop of Eliphalet Chapin, a fine-furniture maker and South Windsor Grant cousin through marriage.

Uncle Ebenezer also earned the commission of captain in 1742, not for his shipping capabilities but for the purpose of leading volunteers from Windsor to the frontiers to fight Indians. He served in the French and Indian War and in the Revolutionary War, commanding the Third Company of Windsor.

The 1758 Ebenezer Grant House, East Windsor Hill, Circa 1858

Commoners, including many of the uncles, aunts, and cousins of the locality, often referred satirically and even sarcastically to their Samuel Grant–associated family kin as the "river gods." The river gods were the captains of local militias that, with the participation of volunteer men of all salient ages, stood on guard and ready to fight for their land and its local investor-governed or self-governed enterprises. Community leaders were the captains and principal investors of enterprises that created wealth. They shared the economic advantages with their risk-free neighbors through providing employment or offering markets for farm produce far and wide.

Trading vessels made the Great River a highway for versatile ships and exotic produce. But the river gods were well connected and became no novices at shoring up worldly goods in the process of providing for their own children and for prosperity and retirement.

Thomas Grant (1692–1769), the only son of Tahan Grant, Jr., became a shoemaker and leather-goods craftsman. Like the Noah Grants of Tolland, the East Windsor cousins were farmers, but they also developed artful auxiliary and profitable trades courtesy of the booming Great River Valley communities at the beginning of the eighteenth century.

In spite of prodigious social differences between them, the Grants were American patriots to a man. East Windsor heirs who followed a father's flourishing higher education opportunities at Yale prepared for gilded careers that went far beyond farming to fill the void as builders of the better-quality homes of the period, as principals of business in shipbuilding, commerce, medicine, law, divinity, and parish philosophy, as elected town and region-wide officials, and eventually as the first elder American statesmen. Some became famous, and we know their reputations, but many, like Ebenezer Grant, are the nearly forgotten unsung leaders and cultural heroes.

Ebenezer lived to be ninety-one years of age. Many of the second and third generations in his particular social group lived comfortably well into the eighth decades of their promising and profitable lives. In terms of career longevity, Ebenezer may have even practiced as a family doctor or the community medicine man for a stretch. A motivated graduate of higher education filled several roles as the most learned man of a community in the eighteenth century. A close cousin of Ebenezer Grant, the Dr. Mathew Rockwell, graduated Yale in 1728, and was able to perform as a spiritual guide in the pulpit on Sunday and be the physician in the East Windsor section of Wapping on weekdays. This particular section of the town was favored for grazing and raising cattle in the early dairy industry, of which Henry Grant is credited with initiating in Wapping. In the nineteenth century, Nathaniel Root Grant, an heir to Henry's local dairy business and a New England contemporary of Jesse Root, peddled his milk with a cart pulled by two oxen from his Wapping farm to shops and homesteads in the extremely marketable East Windsor and South Windsor vicinity.

The local men of the late seventeenth and eighteenth centuries would likely have known, directly and personally, professional elderly compatriots and survivors of the period, like Connecticut lawyers Jesse Root of Coventry and Oliver Ellsworth of Windsor, their elected representatives to the first Continental Congress in 1774. Conversely, these prominent locals had little means to stay in touch with the determined pioneers leaving their home state to go farther west to the frontier. Specifically, once someone left New England, as the third Noah Grant ultimately did, expectations were high that no one would ever see that person or even hear of him again.

Samuel Grant, Sr., and Mary Porter parented seven children. Samuel, Jr., (1659–1710) parented Noah and Ebenezer with Grace Miner of Stonington, Connecticut. The original house, which the father and son had built as one of the first at East Windsor Hill, in 1697, became the back end of a much grander house. The third Noah's uncle Ebenezer actually employed many Grants to build his mansion, including select cousins, nephews and sons.

In good time, the successful Ebenezer had fathered three sons, who became important joiners and skilled craftsmen to the building trades. Aaron (1724–62), Abiel (1729–62), and Alexander (1736–1801), the talented and skilled brothers, practiced the initial carpentry trade by assisting their uncle, the third Noah Grant, in finishing work on his Tolland houses and barns; they simultaneously lessened somewhat their poor uncle's impending debts to prospective creditors.

Ebenezer was the principal for the prodigious house makeover at East Windsor Hill also. The plans for this residence were developed on a sophisticated scale suitable for the merchants of the most influential city of the day, Boston. John Hancock, famous signatory of the Declaration of Independence, lived there in the most magnificent estate house that Ebenezer had visited on business. Patterned after this house, Ebenezer Grant's place became one of the most remarkable houses in Connecticut Colony upon its completion in 1758, at least thirty-three years after the completion of Noah's Tolland house. This 1758 house has been widely known for its decorative "Connecticut Valley doorway." The residence incorporated some of the best construction materials and artisan-handcrafted features and was furnished with goods purchased from early American craftsmen, including cherrywood Chippendale chairs from Eliphalet Chapin.

The direct early colonial-period family of Ulysses S. Grant was one of the few that held cultural and social omnipotence and fortune well beyond any ever seen in Connecticut Colony before. The Grant family also gave more money and manpower than most could provide to support the cause of War of Independence. Mathew Grant, of the Wapping parish, was an example. He led a company of men from Windsor to respond to the Lexington alarm. His gravestone in South Windsor acknowledges his Revolutionary War services to the Fourth Connecticut Company, Nineteenth Regiment. He survived the War and died in 1800. He was a contemporary of his cousin, the third Noah Grant.

Samuel Rockwell Grant (1726–96), the son of Thomas, built a great colonial-period house at Wapping Corners, the intersection of five well-travelled roads. The Wapping parish used this house for services on Sundays before the first church of this section of East Windsor was constructed directly across the road. His son Gustavus (1759–1841) operated a tavern called the Half-Way House in the Samuel Rockwell Grant house at this great intersection between Buckland and Ellington roads. It was well known by travelers as a stopping place for stagecoaches between Boston and New York.

After the Revolutionary War, changes in the route of overland commerce along the Connecticut River increasingly accelerated the decline of the Grant family prosperity and privileges, which had acted to separate them economically and socially from a much larger number of their kin and countryman.

Ebenezer Grant and his son Roswell were the only direct heirs to the power and prestige that Samuel Grant's industry had created in the colony of Connecticut. The third Noah left Connecticut with little to show for his ties to an impressive family, but his great-uncle Ebenezer made very good use of his high standing in the community. Even with the death of his father, Samuel Grant, Jr., in 1710, Ebenezer appointed his widowed mother, Grace Miner, the operator of an elegant inn for over three years at the handsomely furnished East Windsor Hill estate before Ebenezer's son Roswell Grant became its beneficiary.

Jesse Root Grant briefly visited from Ohio in 1833 to settle some family business related to "an uncle's old Connecticut estate." He commented at the time that the Grant residence had obviously seen much better times. He only found three elderly widows living at the house on that occasion, and he told his son, Ulysses, that he simply let them be, settling his interest in the estate for $3,000. The eleven-year-old Ulysses assumed that his father had visited the East Windsor house to settle that estate. He thought that the only Grant family house was located at East Windsor Hill, the only house that his sister would visit at the family reunions in Connecticut. The president and his family never learned of their Grant family estate in Tolland or the story behind it.

Jesse received less than the market value of the one hundred acres and two houses in Tolland Connecticut, but he was more than content to be free of all problems and obligations related to the old place, almost as content as his father, the third Noah, had been when he deserted it for greener pastures in the Connecticut Reserve. When Jesse visited, he must have been very disappointed if he thought he was going to see the East Windsor Hill house and not the one his father had vacated. The Tolland estate had languished in ruin over the many years since his father had left it behind.

I was able to visit the Ebenezer Grant house in 1971. The fate of this house was a different story from the fate of Jesse's father's house. At East Windsor Hill, I met a widow who had graciously answered a letter I had written inquiring about the house at least four years earlier and who kindly showed me the great colonial home's interior before selling it. The magnificence of the workmanship was stunning in all its fine detail, beginning with the overwhelming impact made in the front foyer by the three alternating, distinct styles of handsome decorative staircase railing spindles, which swept with impressive perspective up to the second floor.

Front Reception Area of Ebenezer Grant's 1758 House

The stairway was wide enough for two adults ascending or descending side by side. Exceptional floorboards, which were at least fourteen inches wide, and large double-hung twelve-over-twelves were original, authentic architectural features of the manse. Fine hand-carved woodwork in the wide central hallways and each of the four-over-four large rooms of the main house added a spacious seventeenth- and early eighteenth-century enchantment to wide-open twentieth-century eyes. The craftsmanship was nothing short of 3-D artistic expressionism.

The unrelated woman told some history of the house. It had served as a gentleman's prison for British sympathizers, including Ben Franklin's Tory son, the colonial governor of Virginia. Since enjoying the conversation with her, I have learned of other houses with identical claims attached to them. I still believe that her story is essentially true, since prisoners of the Revolutionary War were moved frequently from one house to another due to obvious security concerns during the War. East Windsor citizens, even the teenage boys with rifles, guarded prisoners throughout the hostilities, moving them often from one house to another or one community to the next. Hessian mercenaries were kept as prisoners at the Grant family house also, as well as at several other homes along the Post Road in Connecticut Colony.

These mercenary soldiers were kept occupied with the task of planting elms and oaks, which grew to be the marvelously massive and beautiful trees that auspiciously still lined the Old Post Road in 1976, two hundred years later, when I, in the prime of my youthful adulthood, studied their physical appearance in awe.

Aaron, Abiel, and Alexander were compensated for their skilled workmanship on the house, as told in the diary of Ebenezer. Aaron and Abiel provided professional carving of moldings and trim. They also worked together later to build Aaron Grant's plain two-story colonial house just across the Boston Post Road from Ebenezer's house. Aaron lived most of his adult life with his immediate family there. Working together with other business and family associates of the building trades, these brothers were contracted to build several additional early colonial-period homes in Connecticut and Massachusetts, particularly in river towns. Some examples of their work can be identified because, like the Ebenezer Grant house of East Windsor, they share the same finely crafted ornate baroque front double doorway that is a significant highlight of the Grant family's work. In successive years, Aaron and Ebenezer Grant partnered as principals in the construction of the first South Windsor church meetinghouse, the third parish house to be built, and they also became principal owners of the burgeoning shipbuilding enterprise located near the family's century-old sawmill.

So it was that the uncle of the third Noah Grant was a fortunate leader in colonial New England. The less notable Noah expected that he would fare more successfully by continuing the family practice of migration westward.

Connecticut Colony had also been an important location for the production of finely handcrafted early American furniture such as the Windsor chair, and it is reasonable to consider that Aaron Grant and his brothers had learned a good deal of their skilled trade from apprenticing with this local industry, just as Erastus Grant, Alexander's son, would eventually do. Virtually for certain, Beldon Grant, a furniture maker, did so. Beldon's specialty was finely crafted chests made from the superior milled materials of local Connecticut cherry, oak, maple, and white pine trees.

The Connecticut River Valley Doorway at East Windsor Hill

Early occupational and career choices were motivated initially by powerful commercial and cultural requirements and the exhilarating effect of the Great River, which provided transport for goods and services all over the world, specifically through contacts with English, French, and Dutch traders. The contrast between the local inland customs, would generally obscure overall an adventuresome worldly bent of the more powerful families. The compelling secret of the powerful was that god had thoroughly blessed the persistent pioneers of industry and commerce who could employ the natural advantages of environmental waterpower. In a few words, god was love and power, for a fortunate few.

The more typical colonial inhabitants, specifically those who had limited access to the Great River, viewed life more in terms of the traditional faith-based scripture that suggested god is wrathful and to be feared and respected, above all. But the few citizens of this valley, who lived in sync with the Great River, perpetually nurtured the more lithe and durable partnership of nature, and made the most of it for blessings of abundance. This grand secret aspect of the "river gods" resonates from the first few generations of Colonial America to the present, and speaks to our generations to come. We know now, as only a few appreciated then the power from natural resources such as sun, wind, and water, and that nature grants unlimited renewable resources (a.k.a. energy). Used wisely for human improvement and progressive environmental advances, our only limits are the present status of our understanding of these durable, and abundant gifts.

Eighteenth-century Chair Belonging to Anne Grant Marsh

CHAPTER 19

Southwest Afterword

Farther West, Ulysses S. Grant, Jr., The US
Grant Hotel, and the Tenor of Peace

As the Civil War ended, a rejoicing Grant proclaimed, "Let us have peace." Ulysses S. Grant wanted a stable peace, but he was also a steadfast promoter of security for the defensible and hard-won liberty for all. He was elected president of the United States due to citizens' trust in his ability to maintain the valued moral and behavioral outcomes as a unified land,

Julia had loved her captivating role as first lady and relished living in the White House for a third term. This shoe fit so well because of her audacious social past as Colonel Dent's southern pampered daughter and her privileged upbringing prior to the War. I have never, though, in all my research about family, found even one Grant who owned slaves, including even our third-generation uncle Ebenezer Grant, but Colonel Dent had enjoyed the services of families of them, as many as sixty people during Julia's years of growing up, and living in the South.

After the Grants' two terms as POTUS and FLOTUS, during which time they influenced from their home at the Executive Mansion, in

Washington, DC, the peace, stability, and a reconstruction of the South, Julia conceded a great longing for their own personal freedom. Ulysses's much expected, but potentially volatile third term as the president was gradually becoming a secondary priority. His companionship to fulfill their wonderful retirement ambitions for worldwide travel was now somehow more urgent. They had also planned a pleasant retirement in San Diego, or somewhere in the far southwest of the country. Julia and the president liked the warm, dry climate that ranged between sixty-eight and eighty-eight degrees at its extremes all year long. They recalled together the welcome natural, cool breezes in San Diego that always wafted by from the Pacific Ocean, at all the most pleasant moments.

The Washington, DC, weather varied greatly with the four seasons and at its coldest ranged between zero and forty-five degrees. Too often, it seemed not so much to their liking, now. And, "Oh my, the dreary clouds and cold rains in the northeast!" she now frequently thought.

A private Grant family railroad car carried Julia with her family to California. Her considerate and dear, "Knight in shinning armor," Ulysses S. Grant was gone, and now just the dearly beloved figment of her memory and imagination. Their son, Ulysses S. Grant, Jr., and Fannie Chaffee Grant, their remarkable daughter-in-law, sat by Julia's side for most of the emotionally and physically draining journey southwest to the coast, and all were hopeful for new adventure. It would be almost two weeks of travel from New York City before they reached what is now Old Town, San Diego, California.

In a much more recent year, 2001, Susan and I drove a "new-to-us," previously loved sedan out there. We were taking a southern route from Connecticut through as many states and diverse American cultures as we possibly could. We had never experienced a trip like this before, in our fifty-six years. In no particular hurry, we enjoyed the leisurely changes in cultures by touring and eating our way through the southern United States. We heartily recommended the crab cakes in North Carolina and the ribs in Tennessee and Texas, to friends and family..

Of course, this trip was only possible since we were both educators, with the whole summer to explore the southern states. Our daughter Heather was planning to fly out in a couple of months to begin what became her now sixteen-year residence in San Diego, where eventually she earned an MSW degree from San Diego State University and began her own family following a lovely wedding to "her man," Michael, on Cape Cod. Airline flights back and forth and here and there across the nation were ubiquitous by the turn of the twenty-first century, and although uncomfortable, they were overwhelmingly preferred to the longer trip on the rails.

Our annual visit to San Diego is now about a month-long family event. It's great to visit with grandkids, Matthew and Calla, and their parents. Michael discovered that the first house they bought held some San Diego family history. The Miners from back east were the original builders and owners of Michael and Heather's home. Someday we must determine the relationship to Grace Miner Grant, her husband Samuel Jr., and the family adventure this heralds.

San Diego has changed so very much since 2001, when Susan and I first crossed the continent. It's impossible to imagine how much since the Grants arrived there in 1893, by train. Ulysses, Jr., and Fannie Chaffee Grant, the daughter of Colorado's first Senator, Jerome B. Chaffee, remained in San Diego permanently and became successful in local real estate enterprises. The boom in development of the city was stimulated, in no small measure, by their activities including the construction of the U. S. Grant Hotel by the year 1910. This was the first luxury hotel to enable city developers, and presidents of the United States alike, to conduct business in the southwestern most American city.

Upon our return to San Diego this year, 2017, we did something I had wanted passionately to do for several years, in more difficult times. Susan and I brought our western family to the U. S. Grant Hotel for dinner. Eight-year-old Matthew seemed the most impressed when the evening manager came to our table to say, "I just noticed your name at the front desk registry. Welcome home, Mr. Grant!" This unexpected, exceptional recognition was surprising, but time seemed to stand still a while as I delighted in it, as did the family. The Grant's Grill Manager went on to offer the informative services of the hotel's head concierge when she heard that I was writing a book about the Grants. For that meeting, I made an appointment on Tuesday of the following week. But we all toasted one another that night in spontaneous excitement about the completion of the book—in just four, and about four hundred years—that evening.

Subsequently, on Tuesday, I did learn truly inspiring facts about the U. S. Grant Hotel from the professional concierge, Mr. Peak, of the wonderful hotel. The Grants opened the doors to the luxury hotel with great celebration October 15, 1910.

"The best and brightest of California society were on hand yearning the success of the hotel and to honor the memory of Ulysses S. Grant, the President of the United States, in whose memory she was built." Originally, $1.9 million was invested to build this landmark, and by 1984 another $80 million had been spent on its first complete restoration. In 2003, the Sycuan Tribal Development Corporation, the business leg of the Kumeyaay Indian Nation, bought the U. S. Grant for $45 million. The second historic restoration was completed in 2006, at a cost of an additional $56 million.

The Kumeyaay Americans made the decision to purchase and restore the U. S. Grant Hotel with exceptional care and concern, since the hotel was built on land their ancestors had originally owned as many as ten thousand years ago. They sought to honor of the memory of President Grant too, as these Native Indians recalled him: "the rare soul among politicians—forthright and generous, he gave them what so many before attempted to take away." As president, Grant had officially recognized the sovereign status of California's Native Indian people and made the executive order to set aside 640 acres of land in East San Diego County, for them.

It is also a sign of honoring General Grant's propriety that so many liberated African Americans expressed appreciation for him by honoring his memory through personally adopting his respectable surname as their own. If a family prodigy like Ulysses S. Grant is any indication of the importance of character and renown, then let us continue to better understand and honor the transmissible principles that he so well signified.

I also recently found, at home in my study, that no fewer than three close members of the family followed the eighteenth president into the US Army. Two of his sons, Fred and Ulysses, 2nd and a grandson, Ulysses S. Grant, 3rd followed his example and became US Generals.

Oh yes! By the way, Ulysses S. Grant, 3rd indicated on his application for membership to the Sons of the American Revolution that his fourth great-grandfather, the third and last Noah Grant, did actually fight though out the Revolutionary War, originally enlisting as a private in a New Hampshire company. He fought throughout the conflict, but just not in Connecticut, as was previously considered by outdated presumption. Even Jesse Grant's old man, with his hardly exceptional mystical suffrage through life, has been inadequately recognized for his bravery over roughly the past 200 years.

A critically inspirational issue of the 1922 Report of the Reunion of the Grant Family Association in Windsor, Connecticut, that was dutifully given as a right of passage by my father, to me, included the speech of Elihu Grant, President and Professor of Pennsylvania's, Haverford College, about evaluating our family traits. His remarks were in part, as follows:

It will, or ought, ever serve the cause of humanity to consider the best of Colonial American character, the fruitage of courage, restraint, and far vision, the inheritance of high ideals of honor and service in the fear of God and the interests of man. By the instinct of kinship we reach for the manners and characteristics we know and have known so well. Thousands of Grants are thus saved in essence and to reflection that will never have a chronicler in print. It is surprising, at first, but inevitable, as we think it over, to note such consistency of traits in the persons whose records are found in our family history. It is equally suggestive to note that these are of the kind of traits that our kindred have remembered and passed on. There is in the record evidence of a genius for steadiness, faithfulness, determination, to carry on the necessary services of life.

Here is the paradox that has never been resolved. Grant the man who wished to be a college professor of mathematics, the citizen craving domesticity, and instinctively magnanimous, has too often been appraised as a bloody exponent of the military ideal of life. Grant the civilian has not yet been clearly discerned because the historians have not enforced upon the popular imagination the study of the man against the background of his kindred, his family of the name. But

we have a man the old-line Americans can admire and love. Crammed with the appreciation of the goodness and greatness of other men, with tenderness, with humor, with common sense, with the vision and judgment going around all sides of a question, an almost superstitious trust in the rightness of things, really a reverence for Providence. Yet he had as few illusions as possible about himself or others. It was Grant the civilian who entered the war. He sought earnestly to save the face of the foe and the soul of the victor by what he considered true manliness. Great elemental forces resided in the strata of centuries of preparation."

U. S. Grant At The End of the Civil War

Previously Unpublished:

Twenty-First-Century Poetry

Life in a Garden

Understanding is in hard reliance on a formative world, the informative world between the atoms and stars.

Persistently the strings of two worlds pull inexplicably toward each other. Together they shape and enhance the other.

She fascinated me, walking in a brilliant light among flowers in the garden. She surprised me with a certain flower in her hair, being so much more stunning than others there.

Among us in a garden something of life flows past the darkness of centuries and their implausible dust. Our light returns to that garden again through twilight, and away in and among the atoms and stars is our endless joy.

Thomas Edward Grant (1973, 2017)

God's Acre Cemetery, South Windsor, CT

Sensibility

There was, as I certainly and clearly remember,
An illumination about that head
A shine about that hair,
And more importantly,
In those eyes
An unmatched essence,
An unmistakable aspect of youthfulness
That expressed love and loveliness.
There was a fascination
In that face and smile,
And in the way I perceived the our becoming,
A fascination of movement and manner that
I was drawn to.

Thomas Edward Grant (1965, 2017)

Intrinsic Acknowledgment

*The oneness
Spans and scans
The structure of
Atoms and stars,
Of
Star men,
Stardust.*

*In the eon
Of fathomless space,
Yes,
One.*

*Stardust
To
Dreams,*

*Traveling
Our Milky-Way!*

Thomas Edward Grant (1997, 2017)

Selected Direct Descendants from
Mathew and Priscilla,
Samuel or Tahan,
GRANT

Generation #	Names of Ancestors
1 Mathew Grant, 1601–81	Priscilla (Grey) Grant, 1601-1644
2 Samuel Grant, 1631–1718	Tahan Grant, 1634–1693
3 Samuel Grant Jr., 1659–1710	Tahan Grant Jr., 1665–1693
4 Noah Grant, 1694–1727	Thomas Grant, 1692–1769
5 Noah Grant Jr., 1718–56	Samuel R. Grant, 1726–1796
6 Noah Grant, third, 1748–1819	Gustavus Grant, 1759–1841
7 Jesse R. Grant, 1794–1873	Wyllys Grant, 1793–1855

8	Ulysses S. Grant, 1822–1885	Norman O. Grant, 1831–1900
9	Ulysses S. Grant. Jr 1852-1929	Louis D. Grant, 1859–1934
10	Ulysses S. Grant, 3rd 1893-1977	Howard L. Grant, 1890–1959
11	Private/Unknown	Howard L. Grant Jr., 1921–2005
12	Private/Unknown	Thomas Edward Grant, 1946-Living

Photography Subject, **Page Number**

SELECTED BIBLIOGRAPHY

~⟁~

Adams, Milton K., and Anthony J. Thoreau. *Old Manchester.*
Manchester, CT: The Manchester Historical Society, 1994.

Avery, Kent C., Donna Siemiatkoski, and Robert T. Silliman.
The Settlement of Windsor, Connecticut. Windsor, CT: The Windsor
Historical Society, 2002.

Brands, H. W. *Ulysses S. Grant in War and Peace.* New York: Anchor
Books, 2013.

Bonekemper, Edward H, III. *Ulysses S. Grant: A Victor, Not A Butcher.*
Washington D.C: Reginery Publishing, 2004.

_____. *The Myth of the Lost Cause.* Washington, DC: Reginery
Publishing, 2015.

Burrows, Edwin G. *Forgotten Patriots.* New York: Basic Books, 2008.

Chamberlain, Samuel, and Henry N. Flynt. *Frontier of Freedom.* New
York: Hastings House, 1952.

Daley, Barney E. *Five Thousand Years At Podunk*. South Windsor: Lithographics, 1985.

_____. *Tobacco Parish: A Collection of South Windsor Memories*. South Windsor: Lithographics, 1998.

Devito, Michael C., and Roger Borrup. *East Windsor Through the Years*. Warehouse Point: The East Windsor Historical Society, 1986.

Flood, Charles Bracelen. *Grant's Final Victory*. Cambridge, MA: Da Capo Press, 2011.

Fowles, Lloyd Wright, and William Joseph Uricchio, *The Fowles History of Windsor Connecticut*. Windsor, CT: Loomis Chaffee Institute, 1976.

Grant, Arthur Hastings, ed. The Grant Family: Report of First Reunion. New York: Press of A.V. Haight, 1899.

Grant, Frank, ed. *The Grant Family: Report of the Fourth Reunion of the Grant Family Association*. Hartford: The Case, Lockwood, and Brainard Co., 1905.

_____. *The Grant Family: Report of the Reunion of the Grant Family Association at the Celebration of the 100th Anniversary of the Birth of Ulysses Simpson Grant*. Westfield, MA, 1922.

Grant, Ulysses S. *Personal Memoirs of Ulysses S. Grant*. New York: Charles L. Webster & Company, 1888.

Grant, Ulysses S, III. *Ulysses S. Grant: Warrior and Statesman*. New York: William Morrow & Company, Inc., 1969.

Isham, Norman M., and Albert F. Brown. *Early Connecticut Houses.* New York: Dover Publications Inc., 1965.

Kelly, J. Fredrick. *Early Domestic Architecture of Connecticut.* New York: Dover Publications, Inc., 1963.

League of Women Voters. *South Windsor Historical Brief and Town Facts.* South Windsor, 1949.

Lewis, Lloyd. *Captain Sam Grant.* Boston: Little, Brown & Company, 1950.

Marshall-Cornwall, James. *Grant as Military Commander.* New York: Barnes & Noble Books, 1995.

McFeely, William S. *Grant.* New York: W. W. Norton & Company, 1981.

Miller, Amelia F. *Connecticut Valley Doorways.* Boston: Boston University Press, 1983.

Perry, Mark. *Grant and Twain.* New York: Random House, 2004.

Porter, Horace. *Campaigning with Grant.* Secaucus, NJ: The Blue and Grey Press, 1984.

Roth, David M., Freeman Meyer. *Connecticut: From Revolution to Constitution.* Chester, CT: The Pequot Press, 1975.

Seifert, Shirley. *Captain Grant.* Philadelphia: J.B. Lippincott Company, 1946.

Schuler, Stanley. Old New England Homes. Pennsylvania: Schiffer Publishing Ltd., 1984.

Silverman, Kenneth. *The Life and Times of Cotton Mather*. New York: Columbia University Press, 1985.

Tercentenary Commission of Connecticut. *The Indians of Connecticut*. New Haven: Yale University Press, 1933.

_____. *Slavery in Connecticut*. New Haven: Yale University Press, 1935

Thistlethwaite, Frank. *Dorset Pilgrims*. London: Barrie & Jenkins, 1989.

Ward, Gerald R., and William N. Hosley Jr., eds. *The Great River*. Hartford: Wadsworth Atheneum, 1986.

Watson, Lois Foster. *The Wapping Five Corners*. East Windsor: Wapping Community Church, 1986.

Waugh, Joan. *U. S. Grant*. Chapel Hill: University of North Carolina Press, 2009.

White, Ronald C. *American Ulysses*. New York: Random House, 2016.

Windsor Historical Society. *Windsor*. Charleston, SC: Arcadia Publishing, 2007

Winik, Jay. *April 1865*. New York: HarperCollins, 2001.

THOMAS EDWARD GRANT OFFERS THE reader a nearly mystical journey paralleling authentic early American concerns and hazards, into an individually death-defying heritage, intently targeted at the Union's potential national civic propriety, and vital decency of moral rank. Wearing the hat of a lyricist-philosopher and poet, Grant is mindful that there is no lasting quarter for one person, no matter how much at-risk, without the herald of a meaningful metaphor, and so writes about the refinement of American physical and spiritual courage through the finer filter of a transcendent, but highly impressive life. Grant examines the life of his distant cousin, Ulysses S. Grant, in the true light of an American family prodigy, and the national hero.

Philosophically committed to accurately observe exigent human scenarios through education and psychology professions, and temperamentally persistent, Thomas committed early in life to achieving a quality education as the most valid and reliable instrument available in the land of his birth, the United States, for the genuine confirmation of individual natural bent, the endowment of talent and intelligent art and science, and life's existential promise. Grant majored as an undergraduate in psychology with the unconventional, but apparently adroitly chosen minor in English literature, and obtained three University of Connecticut (UCONN) degrees: a bachelor's degree in the arts and sciences (1968), a master's in education (1969), and the doctor of philosophy degree (1972).

As an undergraduate student at UCONN, Thom was identified as a particularly promising student for the application of learning theory to the study of educational psychology by professor Joseph S. Renzulli, EdD, graduate of the University of Virginia. Renzulli's mentorship program, Teaching Teachers of the Talented (TTT) granted fellowship through the Congressional National Defense Education Act (NDEA) to counteract institutional racism and unjust discrimination of the opportunity-deprived demographic of middle to late twentieth-century America.

Thomas Edward Grant mindfully processed and integrated his personal and professional experiences with a characteristic examination and reflection that conducted passionate chronicling of the universal personal search for authenticity and attachment. This is achieved through the rendering of illuminating historical details and verse in sympathy and in synch with Grant's own realization of both a career de rigueur and a fulfilling family life. Grant's range of philosophical consideration comes together poignantly through this book about the natural vulnerability of honesty, generosity, humility, valor, kindness, evenhandedness, forgiveness, and arguably the summation of all positive human experiences, boundless gratitude. This comes to a pinnacle in the form of insightful wonder, intuitive questioning, and rewards in the vexing search for relationships, or the normally just-out-of-reach parallels and supporting details of the lives of laudable family antecedents: in this case, the Grants, and their victorious defender of the Union.

APPRECIATION

It is with deepest gratitude that I thank the volunteer and professional associates that are loyal to valid research and the renewal of enlightenment through public and private resources, including local historical societies, colleges and universities, genealogical research facilities, and the countless contributions from those aimed at preserving our national heritages. It is with this assistance, informed guidance, and access to the most genuine resources that we continue to discover and substantiate material for greater historical insights and improved understanding.

In particular, let me acknowledge the following specific public and private organizations that lent a hand and inspiration in this study: the New England Historic Genealogical Society, the Connecticut State Historical Society, the Connecticut State Library, the Windsor Historical Society, and the historical societies of South Windsor and East Windsor, Connecticut. Over the years the collections and exhibits of specific museums have been inspirational and a great resource of continuing value, including the Mark Twain House in Hartford; the Old Mystic Seaport in Mystic, Connecticut; and Old Deerfield and Old Sturbridge Village in Massachusetts. Proceeds from this book will be granted to important institutions like these and also used for the formation of an historical monument in Windsor to honor the origins of the primogenitor of American civil propriety, Ulysses S. Grant.

Finally, one must simply acknowledge with humility and gratitude the credible influence on higher education that the information age, with its ready access to knowledge, brings to substantial research into the true and everlasting.

Thomas Edward Grant

Made in United States
North Haven, CT
15 June 2022

20254431R00138